THE GARDEN
DESIGN
SOURCEBOOK

THE GARDEN DESIGN SOURCEBOOK

THE ESSENTIAL GUIDE TO GARDEN MATERIALS AND STRUCTURES

DAVID STEVENS

Conran Octopus

To Jack Sexton, one of the great landscapers, who has taught
me more details than I care to remember

First published in Great Britain in 1995 by
Conran Octopus Limited
37 Shelton Street
London WC2H 9HN

British Library Cataloguing-in-Publication Data
A catalogue record for this book is available from the British Library.

ISBN 1 85029 7320

Illustrations by Vanessa Luff

Art Editor: Tony Seddon
Project Editor: Kate Bell
Text Editor: Caroline Taylor
Picture Research: Nadine Bazar, Julia Pashley
Illustration Visualization: Lesley Craig
Production: Julia Golding

Index by Indexing Specialists, Hove, East Sussex

Printed and Bound by Milanostampa, Italy

Contents

DESIGN
CONSIDERATIONS

Good garden design is essentially simple and fit for its purpose. Great gardens display these basic qualities, but show in addition a subtle and apparently instinctive ability to link with the house they adjoin, and the environment in which they are placed.

Beyond this, there are practical factors that have to be taken into account. One of these is that we live in a world in which new technologies, materials and ideas are continually coming on to the market, which affect gardens and garden design as much as any other field.

You only have to observe the enormous array of surfacing, products, ornaments and furnishings available at any garden centre, nursery or builder's yard today to see how easily overcomplication, which is the antithesis of good design, can become a problem. We are seduced by what catches our eye, and it is little wonder that so many garden compositions end up as an unrelated mass of features, materials and design ideas, in dramatic contrast to well thought out, simpler affairs that work so much better.

The problem is largely an historical one. Until comparatively recent times, whole areas were built and laid out in vernacular style, using local materials, and this produced a feeling of harmony and of locality. It is respect for the vernacular and for the immediate environment that makes the majority of period gardens look so right and comfortable. Only recently have transportation systems allowed materials and people to be moved around the country quickly and easily. As a result, fine stone or hand-made brick from one area can end up in a garden in quite a different locality, and although it may look superb in its own setting – or even in isolation – it may appear decidedly uncomfortable in relation to the traditional local materials found around it.

Ease of transportation is also linked to cost-effectiveness; whatever their source, materials can now be cheaply and competitively priced. Many modern materials are also more durable than traditional ones, as well as being cost-effective and good to look at, which all means that the dividing

Good garden design is often impossible to define, but this composition certainly achieves it. A combination of stability and continuity is shown in both the hard and soft landscape materials, as well as being reflected in the superb use of perspective and the focal point at the end of the vista. Control is perhaps the most important tool at the designer's disposal.

Simplicity is the key to all good design, whatever the field, and in this composition, with its strong Japanese overtones, such a philosophy is clearly demonstrated in the impeccably styled floor, walls and decking, all of which relate perfectly to one another.

line between a restrained and sensible choice, and the introduction of too many varied and tempting elements, is a narrow one.

Visual confusion or incompatibility of this kind is often compounded by our readiness to travel to the four corners of the world. From these trips we bring back design ideas that have made a strong impression on us. While all this may widen our range of choice, it is, to all but the strongest-willed, an invitation to overcomplication! I cannot stress often enough the prime rule of good garden design: simplicity and fitness of purpose, geared to a respect for the garden's surroundings.

However, the wide range of available materials can be a positive asset, as long as these materials are carefully chosen to complement a scheme, or match surfaces or artifacts already in the garden. You most certainly can mix and match materials,

The invitation to step outside should be a strong one and the elements here achieve that ideal, from the decked porch, which links with the floorboards inside the house, to the carefully chosen weathered seat. The subtle relationship between the paving and planting provides a comfortable balance that is characteristic of much good design.

This garden epitomizes the vernacular style at its best, using a combination of local materials and patterns to produce a design that is in perfect harmony not only with its immediate surroundings, but also with the wider landscape. There is a direct visual link between the cobbles, the clipped balls and the regular shape of trees in the distance.

but to do so effectively and sympathetically you must understand their characteristics and the way they relate to each other. This has to do with a feeling of 'rightness' that is one of the good designer's most valuable tools.

When I teach my students I do not talk straight away about garden design. Indeed, I positively discourage them from thinking about gardens at first, and emphasize the point that garden design relates to all the other design disciplines. We look first at the environment, analysing the street scene, discussing the merits of architectural style, and looking at as many different design disciplines as possible. I point out that many of the greatest architects, such as Sir Edwin Lutyens or Frank Lloyd Wright, were complete designers in that they created the house, landscape, furniture, floor coverings, cutlery, and everything else to do with a particular environment. I also make the point that anyone can look at design in this all-embracing, practical, way and that doing

so brings an understanding that encourages respect and restraint when using materials.

In some gardens the choices will be obvious: no one, I hope, would think of laying blue, pink and red precast concrete paving slabs outside a fine old stone cottage. The logical choice here would be a similar stone, a matching gravel, or perhaps mellow brick – depending on what is used locally. All these materials are of a kind, and as they belong to the same genetic and visual family they look and feel comfortable together.

Problems arise when there is no strong local identity: on a new housing estate or development, or in the heart of town where building styles have been thrown together over a long period of time. Yet even here there will be clues and guidelines. A rendered concrete and colour-washed suburban building might look fine with crisp grey paving and well detailed raised beds built from railway ties or sleepers; a dark courtyard garden in town might successfully be floored with reflective white

This superb composition certainly qualifies as an outside room. Floors, walls and ceilings can be furnished and clothed in an infinite number of ways.

chippings teamed with polished black slate. Such settings could be contained with well-detailed fences or other boundary treatments; subtly furnished with pots and ornaments; framed with overheads; and punctuated with focal points.

In small gardens, where more of the space is often visible at one time, the creative process needs to be especially restrained, to ensure that the various elements are all 'of a kind'. In a larger garden the area could be divided into separate 'rooms', each with a different theme or purpose, but even here there must be a broad overview of the entire composition to ensure that the different components harmonize one with another, with the property they adjoin, and with the setting.

It is a fact that while many people are perfectly competent to plan the interior of their homes, and display sound commonsense in doing so, their ideas often go haywire once they move outside.

The excitement of discovery is experienced here by the need to pass from one area to the next, through the tension point of the gate and on towards the bench.

Tension, mystery and surprise are key elements in garden design and an area that can be seen in its entirety at a single glance is far less attractive than one that is divided into different spaces, each with its own individual character. A curving path that disappears from view always provides a delicious invitation to explore the places beyond.

Providing each space within the garden with its own individual theme encourages you to pause for enjoyment before passing on to the next. A garden that is filled with such areas will naturally feel larger than it really is, because you cannot see the whole composition and it will take some time to move through each area.

The inherent characteristics of the site, and the position of a feature within the garden, will frequently be the major factors that determine the final appearance of a particular area. This three-layered boundary displays tremendous strength of purpose.

Plants can be just as architectural as bricks and mortar, and there is enormous stability in these clipped yew buttresses that emphasize the softer planting in between.

This is mainly because most of us see the house and garden as separate entitities, and treat them as such. If, on the other hand, we think of inside and out as a single living environment then we will choose garden materials and furnishings that are compatible both with the house and its setting.

This is the crux of what total design is all about: it is the realization that everything that surrounds us is interrelated. In today's world very little, including the landscape, exists without the touch or interference of man. Poor design is always poor; but objects, materials and systems that are well conceived will always relate to one another in an entirely sympathetic way.

None of what I have said so far tells you how to design a garden; that is not the brief of this book. Whether a composition is formal, asymmetric or informal is immaterial. What is important is how to use and respect the materials at your disposal, so that they relate to one another, to the garden as a whole, and to the setting at large, and by so doing ensure that the overall design is coherent.

That house and garden should be closely related, both visually and physically, is irrefutable, as is the idea that the garden should be looked upon as a series of rooms, each with a different

purpose or theme. How these rooms are used and arranged will be determined by your personality, and the needs of your family; linking these spaces into the surrounding landscape will be a fulfilling experience. My role is to ensure you get the components and details right to enable you to carry out your own ideas. Once the mechanics are understood, the rest will follow naturally.

Refer to the Glossary on page 184 for explanations of terms used in the book.

KEY TO SYMBOLS

COST

cheap   medium-priced   expensive

EASE OF USE

straightforward   moderate   complicated

DURABILITY

short-term   medium-term   long-term

FLOORS

To be effective, floors need to be well laid and visually attractive. In this composition, a simply planted bed, exposed aggregate slabs and bands of carefully laid cobbles are enclosed in a framework of brick paving.

The floor, whether formed of hard or soft landscaping, is one of the most important elements in the garden, often acting as a framework to the entire composition. Hard landscaping will provide paths, surfacing for utility areas, steps, ramps, driveways and parking areas for vehicles, room for sitting and dining, and many other incidental features. In terms of cost, it may account for up to seventy-five per cent of your total garden budget, so it makes sense to choose carefully and to ensure that it is laid or built to last. A well-laid floor should last a lifetime, making it doubly important to choose the right design; mistakes or a change of mind will be expensive to correct.

One of the most important considerations when designing a garden is the allocation of a sensible budget, which can be phased over as long a period as you want. The kind of floor you choose will naturally affect the cost, and as a general rule, natural materials are more expensive than man-made ones. Your choice will be determined first and foremost by the basic design

and character of the garden, and this in turn will be influenced by the style, location and age of the adjoining house, as well as by your own personality and lifestyle.

A brick house, for example, may encourage you to consider using a similar-coloured brick in the garden, probably teamed with a complementary material (perhaps a natural stone or a neat, precast concrete slab). A single type of paving may look visually 'heavy' for a whole terrace or sitting area near the house, but bear in mind that too many different materials have an unsettling effect. Overcomplication is the antithesis of good design, and two surfaces used to complement each other are often just right, the one balancing and perhaps softening the other. You will find that one surface tends to become the dominant partner, with the second used as a framework, as panels, or as highlights within the overall area.

Larger, less intimate spaces, on the other hand, such as driveways or parking areas, are more restful if constructed from a single material, perhaps gravel or concrete blocks. Both these will need containing or edging in some way, and edgings can also play an important role in containing or separating plants within a paved area. The choice of a compatible 'trim' is vitally important, and as a general rule, any edging should be simple but impeccably detailed.

While the visual implications of any hard landscaped area are extremely important, so, too, is the way in which the surface is constructed; it is this that will guarantee a long life, and ensure the safety of those using the space. Poorly detailed steps, for example, are dangerous, as are paving slabs that are simply bedded on sand; they will settle to form an uneven surface, inviting someone to trip.

Any paved area will need proper foundations, and these will range from something relatively simple for heavy materials such as paving stones or railway sleepers, to an altogether more solid base for smaller modules that move easily or that must sustain heavy wear and tear. The condition of the ground underneath will obviously have an effect on foundations, and the softer this is, the deeper the foundations will need to be. The standard base for most paving is well-compacted hardcore or crushed stone, a minimum of 100mm (4in) thick, over which can be laid a mortar bed that will accept the slabs or surface in question. If there are gaps in the surface after the hardcore or crushed stone has been laid and compacted, it should be covered or 'blinded' with smaller material, such as finely crushed stone, to ensure an even surface for the mortar.

Drainage is another consideration; any surface needs to shed water quickly after rain, and flooring will need to slope or 'fall' away from the house, usually to a minimum gradient of 1:100. Water can often be directed into a planted area or lawn, but sometimes, as in the case of a courtyard or sunken area, a drain, or series of drains, will have to be installed beneath the paved area, and the latter angled towards them. In temperate climates where a damp proof course is required to prevent moisture from percolating up walls, the finished surface of any adjoining paving should fall at least 150mm (6in) below this.

Paving is usually used on a single plane, but virtually all the various options will also be suitable for steps and ramps. Here, sound construction is vital, and any flight should be as wide and as generous as possible. Ideal dimensions for steps use a 150mm (6in) riser, and a 450mm (18in) tread. Steps in an informal part of the garden may be larger and more easy-going, and in some situations steps, or large interlocking platforms, can occupy virtually the whole garden.

Timber, which is another important hard surface, entails straightforward carpentry skills. Decking is popular in many of the drier and sunnier parts of the world, but is under-used in more temperate climates, which is a pity; as long as adequate ventilation is provided underneath, and the timber treated with preservative, its life can be long and useful. Timber can also be used as logs, log slices, sleepers, or wood chips, any of which can have their place in the overall garden design.

Of course, large areas of the garden can often be given over to soft surfacing, and although this will take rather longer to establish than hard, it will usually be far more cost-effective. Here again, sound preparation (this time in the form of good topsoil and thorough cultivation) is essential. Whether such surfaces are grass, low ground covers that form a carpet, drifts of wild flowers, or sweeps of bulbs, will depend on their position within the overall design.

In the final analysis, you should remember that the floor essentially serves as a background for the widest possible range of activities. It should not, therefore, dominate the design, but should rather provide a subtle understatement into and around which the boundaries and planting of the garden can be woven.

A patchwork of broken paving materials gives an inherently 'busy' design, which can often clash with the cleaner lines of an adjoining house. This path, however, is so well laid, with its carefully chosen stones and impeccably laid pieces of tile, that the whole composition becomes a work of art.

NATURAL STONE

Characteristics: Natural sandstone, of which York stone is a typical example, is found all over the world. It displays a wonderful range of subtle colours and textures, and it is this variation that makes it one of the finest and most sought-after paving materials. It is generally expensive.

Uses: This fine paving stone is perfect for seating areas, paths and terraces. It can be supplied new, sawn into slabs of virtually any size, or second-hand, when it is often reclaimed from street pavements or the floors of old mills and factories. If this is the case, it should be carefully checked, as it may contain oil that will sweat out in hot weather, resulting in an oily mess.

Natural stone is sometimes available in very thin slabs, but these are likely to be insufficiently durable for use outside. Broken stone, because of its inherently 'busy' nature, is best used in informal parts of the garden, or contained within a grid of brick or granite setts.

Laying: Slabs are normally supplied in random-sized rectangles, ranging from 900 x 600mm (36 x 24in) to 300 x 300mm (12 x 12in), and these should be laid around a small central keystone. Slabs will be of uneven thickness, and foundation levels must accommodate this. They should be bedded on a weak, semi-dry mortar mix to a minimum gradient of 1:100. They can either be neatly pointed, with the joints slightly rubbed back, or left open and filled with sifted soil so that low-growing plants can be seeded in. The occasional small slab can be omitted, and the space either planted, or infilled with a contrasting material such as brick or cobbles.

Contrasting & associating materials: Brick, granite setts, cobbles, gravel.

Natural stone quickly acquires a patina of age, with mosses and lichens colonizing the surface to produce a rich texture. The joints between slabs can be deliberately left open and filled with a little sifted soil, allowing plants such as Alchemilla *and* Verbascum *to self seed.*

LAYING NATURAL STONE

Natural stone differs in size and thickness. Compensate by laying slabs on varying depths of mortar over a 100mm (4in) layer of hardcore.

Slabs arranged around a keystone

Slabs

Mortar

Well-compacted hardcore

Well-compacted soil

These stone steps have an informal character that is both rugged and physically strong. The gentle curve of the flight naturally provides a feeling of movement that draws you inevitably up towards the higher level.

Natural sandstone paving is the finest paving material you can lay, having a great feeling of permanence and displaying subtle colour variations. Random rectangular slabs are ideal for terraces and pathways, and this naturally architectural surface can be amply softened by adjacent planting that is allowed to flop over the edges.

GRANITE

Granite setts provide a durable and informal paving material that is ideal for paths in many parts of the garden. Because of their small size, setts can easily be laid to a curve. If the joints are left open, low-growing plants can be allowed to colonize.

Characteristics: Granite is a hard, igneous rock, found throughout the world. It is usually speckled in appearance, and can range in colour from pink, through brown to black. It has long been used in areas of heavy wear such as street paving, and was often laid in fan-shaped patterns.

Uses: Like sandstone, granite can be sawn into slabs, when it is incredibly expensive, but is more often seen as small rectangular paving blocks known as setts. Full setts are roughly the size of a brick; half setts are cube-shaped. Their surface is slightly uneven, making them ideal for paths, driveways, ramps and edgings, but less suitable for sitting areas.

Granite setts associate well with many other natural materials, and their small modular size allows them to be laid easily to curves or to form patterns. They can often be used as a frame for other materials, such as an edging for tarmac on a driveway, or to subdivide areas of brushed aggregate concrete. Setts are effective used in courses around a tree or smaller planting in an area of gravel.

Laying: Setts should be firmly set as closely as possible in a bed of mortar over a layer of well-compacted hardcore, and should be selected from the stack by hand, so that irregularities can be matched and minimized. If laying to a pattern, draw the pattern to scale first, marking any changes of direction, trims, and other pertinent details. This will allow you to work accurately, and will help you to estimate the quantity of setts required.

Contrasting & associating materials: Sandstone, gravel; as trims or edgings, with concrete or tarmac.

FULL SETTS LAID IN A STRETCHER BOND

HALF SETTS LAID IN FAN SHAPES

LAYING GRANITE SETTS
To lay granite setts, bed them in mortar as tightly together as possible over a layer of compacted hardcore.

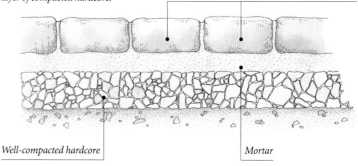

Tightly packed granite setts

Well-compacted hardcore

Mortar

Sawn and polished granite, although expensive, makes a superb paving material. Because of its great strength, it can be sawn into relatively thin tiles; the interlocking pattern shown on this roof garden produces a real feeling of movement.

SLATE

MARBLE

When split into small pieces and laid loose, slate can be used as a pathway or ground cover. Like gravel, it crunches loudly underfoot, lending it the added attraction of being a useful burglar deterrent. Here it is used successfully in a naturalistic setting.

This stunning example of intricate paving shows craftsmanship at its best. Square marble slabs are subdivided by tiny patterned tiles which are perfectly aligned with the surrounding edging. This kind of scheme needs to be carefully thought out before the work starts.

Characteristics: Slate is a sedimentary rock found throughout the world. It is usually dark grey in colour, and splits easily along its bedding plane.

Uses: Slate is an ideal paving material. The dark colour associates well with lighter materials: when wet it becomes glossy, throwing it into sharper relief. However, it does absorb heat, which can make paving alarmingly hot to bare feet! Slate can be sawn into rectangles to produce a crisp, finish; broken into 'crazy' or 'random' pieces which can be carefully laid and pointed; or broken into even smaller pieces and used loose as pathways, or as ground cover through which planting can be grown. Roof slates can be set on edge as paving, and although expensive, the end result is superb. Slate is also used as coping for some traditional walls, as a damp proof course, or as a creasing course beneath coping, to prevent moisture percolating up or down garden walls.

Laying: Slate paving needs to be firmly bedded in mortar over a well-consolidated layer of hardcore or crushed stone, to prevent it snapping.

Contrasting & associating materials: Light-coloured chippings and gravel, pale-coloured precast paving, pale-coloured bricks, stone paving.

Characteristics: Marble is a relatively hard sedimentary rock with wide colour variations and a veined surface. Good quality stone is often difficult to find, which makes it an unusual, expensive and often stunning choice for the right garden.

Uses: This high-cost, dramatic surface is best used as sawn and polished slabs in up-market architectural schemes, perhaps linked to a similar floor inside the house. Its reflective qualities and pale colour can help to brighten a dark area, but marble must be used with sensitivity to avoid vulgarity, particularly in the softer light of temperate countries. Broken marble, used as random or crazy paving, should be avoided. Courses or panels of polished slate can be used to provide a superb, if glitzy, counterpoint to marble slabs.

Laying: Marble slabs are usually of even thickness and should be bedded on mortar over a well-compacted layer of hardcore or crushed stone. They can either be butt-jointed as closely as possible, or laid slightly further apart with deeply raked joints to emphasize the surface.

Contrasting & associating materials: Slate or other dark stones, including dark grey precast concrete slabs.

COBBLES & BOULDERS

The visual power of these huge boulders is immense and they offer the perfect counterpoint to the simple adjoining architecture and the thick rendered garden walls. Large rocks can be difficult to move so it is best to incorporate them into your design where they are found.

LAYING A COBBLE PATH
Lay cobbles tightly together so that no mortar is visible between each stone.

Tightly packed cobbles

Wooden peg

Wooden board

Well-compacted hardcore

Mortar

Characteristics: In general, cobbles are small and boulders large, but both are rounded, water-worn stones from river beds or the beach. (Incidentally, in many countries it is illegal for private individuals to take them away from the coast.) Cobbles and setts are often confused, but where setts are always rectangular or square, most cobbles are egg-shaped. Colour will vary, according to source, from almost black, through blue-grey, to pale grey and white.

Uses: Cobbles were, and still are in certain parts of the world, used for street and pedestrian paving, where they are often found in beautifully laid patterns. They form an uneven surface and are therefore ideal where grip is needed, on a sloping path or drive. They are, on the other hand, usually unsuitable for paved areas where furniture is likely to be used.

Cobbles usually look best laid as simply as possible, using a single colour and size, and packed as closely together as possible so that no mortar is visible between the joints. In larger paved areas, they can be used in panels or courses to form a contrast to other surfaces, to divide a space, or to surround and highlight a specific feature such as a tree. Very small cobbles often look better than a large wedge of mortar between the joints of a curved path.

Laid loose, their character is completely different. Here, they can be piled up as a textured ground-cover, either in areas where planting will not grow, or as an excellent counterpoint to foliage. Difficult areas, such as manholes, can be easily disguised with a combination of loose cobbles, larger boulders and ground cover planting, all of which can be eased carefully out of the way if access is needed.

Boulders associate well with cobbles, and can also provide sculptural interest if used in isolation. At their largest, perhaps a metre or several feet in diameter, boulders can act as dramatic focal points, and can be positioned within a planted area or set in paving to act as occasional seats. Used in groups, they provide a physical deterrent, guiding both feet and eye through a space, or acting as a pivot at the turn of a path.

Cobbles and boulders associate particularly well with water. Cobbles can be used as a beach at the edge of a shallow pool or pond, and boulders can be drilled to allow water to flow up and over the surface. Both make far safer water features for children than an open area of water.

Laying: Where cobbles are to be walked on, they should be laid as closely together as possible, and bedded in mortar over a base of well-consolidated hardcore. If used loose, within a planted area, they can be placed over a base of weak concrete, black plastic sheeting, or a porous geo-textile. All will prevent weed growth from contaminating the area.

Boulders can either be laid loose, or bedded in mortar if they are set within a paved area where they are to be used for sitting, children's play, or as a sculptural feature.

Contrasting & associating materials: Both associate well with virtually any other surface, whether natural or man-made.

Cobbles are traditionally laid in intricate patterns which can engender a great sense of movement through an area. Here the pattern is reminiscent of a carpet and is carried in a long, elegant strip down the flight of steps, leading the eye round the corner of the building.

SAND

Raked sand in Japanese gardens is often used to represent a stretch of water. Here, large rocks are positioned in the sand to indicate islands in the middle of an ocean. This composition is a superb study in the texture of different materials.

Characteristics: The dividing line between gravel, grit and sand is a moot point; the finer gravel becomes, the closer it is to sand. Like gravel, sand comes in a wide range of colours and grades.

Uses: Fine sand is really only suited to children's play areas, and for this 'silver sand' is the only satisfactory type; unlike the yellow builder's variety, it does not stain. The coarser types of sand may be used for a raked surface in gardens with a Japanese influence. However, the symbolism of Japanese gardens is probably best left to the Japanese, and it is generally more sensible to use a fairly straightforward pattern of raking rather than attempting to imitate the intricacies of the genuine article.

Laying: All sands and grits should be laid either over a weak mix of concrete or over a geo-textile membrane. The finished depth need not be great, 50–70mm (2–3in) is quite sufficient, but sand provides an ideal medium for the germination of weeds, and these will need to be attended to at regular intervals.

Contrasting & associating materials: Smooth, water-worn stones and boulders. Also looks superb with darker shades of timber decking.

GRAVEL, CHIPPINGS & HOGGIN

Characteristics: Gravel and chippings are both made up of small stones. As a general rule, gravel consists of rounded stones, while chippings are angular. Sizes vary from a few millimetres across, to approximately 12mm (½in). Hoggin is a binder consisting of clay and gravel extracted from the same pit, and is often used as a base for the first two, or by itself with a top-dressing of gravel. The colour and texture of these materials varies enormously.

Uses: These materials are frequently used for cost-effective paths and drives in both town and country. Being a 'fluid' module, they can be laid in strong, flowing curves that give a real feeling of space and movement. The colour of the gravel or chippings can be chosen to link with adjoining stone or brickwork, and paler colours used to reflect light in shady or dark areas – especially in urban basements or courtyard gardens. Gravel and chippings can provide a natural foil for planting allowed to grow through the surface, and will act as a mulch, retaining moisture in the ground.

Laying: The way in which gravel or chipping paths and driveways are laid is critical; a surface that washes about when driven over or is a struggle to walk across is quite unacceptable. Well-constructed surfaces that are firm underfoot can last over a hundred years but two things are essential: thorough compaction at every stage of laying and edge restraints that prevent the surface from moving outwards. Edging can range from timber boards, firmly

pegged in position, to bricks haunched (set) in concrete.

Laying a driveway is best left to a professional, who will ensure that the foundation and base course uses the correct size of stone and is thoroughly rolled. Foundations for a driveway, which takes more wear than a path, need to be a minimum of 150mm (6in). The top wearing course of hoggin is laid to a slight camber so that it sheds water easily, preventing puddles forming, which would quickly undermine the surface. The final top dressing of gravel will be just enough to cover the surface, and is rolled into dampened hoggin, which will act as a binder.

Gravel and hoggin paths are laid in much the same way, but with shallower foundations. Chippings are also laid over a firm and well-compacted base of hardcore or crushed stone, but the surface is left looser, to form a decorative element rather than a hard-wearing surface.

Loose gravel used as a foil to planting can be laid over a weak mix of concrete with gaps left for planting pockets, or over a sheet of geo-textile which has been pierced to allow plants to grow through. Such areas can be allowed to run off into surrounding beds and do not need a firm edge restraint.

Contrasting & associating materials: All associate with the widest possible range of both hard and soft landscape surfaces and features, and can be matched for colour, or used as a definite contrast (e.g. honey-coloured gravel with a golden sandstone; or white chippings in sharp relief to polished black slate).

White chippings make a useful ground cover and provide an attractive foil to planting, which can be allowed to grow through the surface. Their ability to reflect light means they can be invaluable when used to brighten a dark courtyard or basement garden.

LAYING A GRAVEL PATH
Always lay gravel paths to a slight camber to allow water to drain off easily. Thorough compaction is necessary at all stages of the job and firm edge restraints are essential.

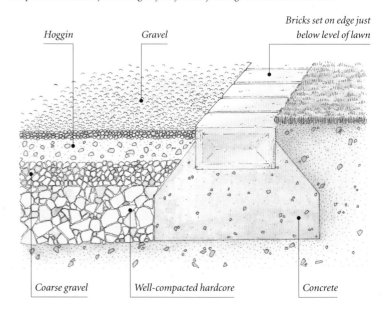

Hoggin *Gravel* *Bricks set on edge just below level of lawn*

Coarse gravel *Well-compacted hardcore* *Concrete*

This path is a pure work of art. It would take a great degree of determination to walk over the surface and disturb that beautifully raked pattern! It is an impeccable study in the contrast between different surfaces, the visual softness of the gravel complementing the stability and power of the natural stone slabs within a neat framework of grass.

DECKING

Characteristics: Timber decking is one of the most useful hard landscape materials available and, provided construction is carried out correctly, can be used anywhere in the world and expect a long and durable life. With the decimation of many tropical rain forests, it is worth checking that the timber comes from a renewable source.

Decking may be constructed from hardwood or softwood. Colours and graining provide a wonderful diversity of choice, and can be chosen to link with an adjoining wooden building or interior floor. Decking made from hardwood will need minimal maintenance, whereas softwood should be pressure-treated before it is used or treated regularly with non-toxic preservative.

Decking is a versatile material that is ideal for extending a horizontal surface out over a slope, in this case forming a roof terrace. Because timber is so easy to cut, it can be customized to fit the most awkward sites and shaped to fairly complex patterns. The timber can also be carried through the design to form handrails and other similar details.

CONSTRUCTING DECKING

Decking forms an ideal extension from the house, particularly when there is sloping ground. The direction of the boards will provide extra visual emphasis.

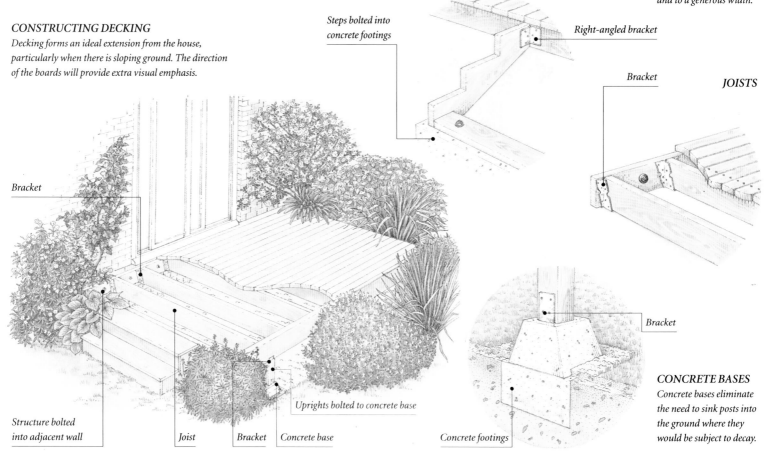

Steps bolted into concrete footings

STEPS
Construct steps soundly and to a generous width.

Right-angled bracket

Bracket

JOISTS

Bracket

Bracket

Structure bolted into adjacent wall

Joist   *Bracket*   *Concrete base*

Uprights bolted to concrete base

Concrete footings

Bracket

CONCRETE BASES
Concrete bases eliminate the need to sink posts into the ground where they would be subject to decay.

Uses: Decking is particularly valuable where a garden slopes away from the house, enabling a series of decks, linked by steps, to provide flat surfaces adjacent to the building. Decks can also be used around water features or swimming pools, as barbecue areas, or to form boardwalks through woodland. Seats, rails, steps, overheads, tubs and other features can easily be incorporated as required. Decking is particularly suited to sites where load-bearing is a problem, such as roof gardens and balconies. Additionally, it can be cut into virtually any shape, echoing the lines of adjoining architecture, or allowing established trees to grow through the surface.

Construction: Any competent carpenter can build decking, using straightforward skills. Adequate ventilation is essential, especially in wetter climates; there should be a minimum clearance from the ground of 150mm (6in). A framework of joists is bolted to uprights concreted into the ground. Boards are then nailed or screwed on to the joists, and a strong visual emphasis can be determined by the direction in which these boards run in relation to the house or immediate surroundings. Wide boards tend to make a space feel smaller, whereas narrow ones make it feel larger. Boards of different widths set up an interesting rhythm. Whatever their size, make sure spacing is regular, and not so wide as to trap spike heeled shoes.

On a roof garden, a lighter supporting framework of 50 x 50mm (2 x 2in) timbers is set on shims (thin wedges) to level the surface, and care must be taken not to obstruct drainage. Boards are then nailed to the framework, and these can be set diagonally or at right angles to the main building, or in small chequerboard panels.

Contrasting & associating materials: A house built of the same material, woodland settings, and timber such as railway sleepers; in a contemporary setting, decking looks handsome when placed near brushed aggregate paving, gravel, or *in situ* concrete walling.

Boardwalks make attractive features and are particularly successful when sited close to water, where they can be shaped to complement the curve of a bank. They should be set on solid timber piles driven into the surrounding ground. Water-resistant hardwood, such as elm, is ideal for the latter or, alternatively, you could use concrete posts.

Timber boards possess a strong architectural line that will draw the eye in a particular direction. They also weather beautifully, the slightly harder grain in the wood gradually becoming exposed and standing out in relief to form a rich surface patina. Timber furniture is the most logical choice for extending the theme.

RAILWAY SLEEPERS & LOGS

Logs can be used to form attractive and durable paths and steps, particularly in an informal or woodland setting. Remove any bark from the timber to minimize the chances of rot setting in. Soften the line of the path by encouraging adjacent planting to flop over the edges. Additional planting can be seeded into the joints between each log.

Characteristics: Railway sleepers (known in the United States as railway ties) measure approximately 2.5m x 200mm x 130mm (8ft x 8in x 5in); logs may be any size. Either will form a powerful element in any composition. Sleepers are usually pine and, as they have been treated with preservative, rarely need any further protection. It is important to select clean ones, as many are contaminated with oil which may sweat out during hot weather. Logs can be hardwood or softwood and are usually untreated; however, it is possible to buy bark-stripped and pressure-treated logs of a specific diameter: these are regular in shape and more architectural in nature.

Uses: Railway sleepers make fine paths, steps, raised beds and paving, though the slightly uneven surface may not make them suitable for positioning tables and chairs. Both sleepers and logs can be used for steps; treads and risers can abut one another, or wider treads can incorporate a range of surfaces such as chipped bark, gravel, or – in a more architectural setting – paving of various kinds. Steps can be straight. or informally staggered, with planting softening the edges.

Laying/Construction: Because of the heavy weight of logs and sleepers, solid foundations are usually unnecessary. For paving, a foundation of well-compacted soil is normally adequate. They should then be bedded close together on a 50mm (2in) layer of sifted soil to allow for levelling. No fall is necessary, as water can drain away freely between them.

For steps on a shallow slope, sleepers and logs can often be bedded directly into cut-outs in the bank. On a steeper gradient, it may be necessary to peg the risers with wooden stakes (set behind the risers to hide them) or drill the timbers and drive metal rods vertically at least 600mm (24in) into the ground. Treads can be formed either from another sleeper, set behind the riser, or from another compatible surface. Where logs are used, they should have a diameter of at least 150mm (6in), and be firmly pegged in position. As edging for an informal path through a level area, the logs can be partially buried in the ground.

Contrasting & associating materials: Railway sleepers: virtually all other hard landscape materials, such as precast concrete slabs, gravel, stone chippings or brushed aggregate, especially those in a contrasting colour. In less formal situations: chipped bark, gravel or hoggin.

Railway sleepers can be used to construct relaxed and easy-going steps that are ideal in an informal part of the garden. Well-compacted gravel is a good choice for treads and a series of terracotta pots have been used to reinforce the visual impact of the flight.

CONSTRUCTING LOG STEPS

Log steps are ideal in an informal setting. Risers of unequal lengths will merge naturally into any adjacent planting.

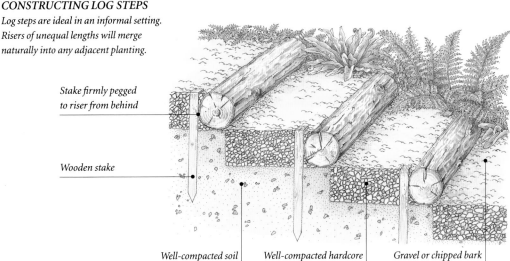

Stake firmly pegged to riser from behind

Wooden stake

Well-compacted soil

Well-compacted hardcore

Gravel or chipped bark

LOG SLICES

Log slices of an irregular size can be laid to form a rich, almost abstract, surface texture that is full of interest. These have been bedded into a layer of fine gravel, the pale colour throwing the timber into sharp relief.

Natural materials blend perfectly into a natural situation and always look far better in such places than precast concrete slabs or natural stone. Provided they are sufficiently thick, hardwood slices will last a remarkably long time.

Characteristics: Log slices consist of discs sawn from the trunks of trees. Hardwoods are the best choice as they last longest. Slices need to have a minimum diameter of 450mm (18in) and to be at least 150mm (6in) thick.

Uses: Usually laid informally as stepping stones through a wild area, through woodland or through planting. They can sometimes be used to form an informal paved area, butted together as tightly as possible, with wood chips filling the joints.

Laying: Log slices are laid directly on to soil excavated to a depth of 150mm (6in) before being levelled and compacted. Lay stepping stones on the ground and try out the distance between them for comfort before bedding them in. Staggering the line of the path creates the most naturalistic effect. If the area is shady and the wood likely to become slippery as a result, you can staple chicken wire to the surface to improve the grip.

Contrasting & associating materials: Usually best on their own, or to link areas of wooden decking or railway sleepers; associate well with wood chips and gravel.

CHIPPED BARK

The informal character of chipped bark makes it ideal for constructing low cost and surprisingly durable paths in a naturalistic setting. It associates particularly well with planting but a certain degree of ongoing maintenance will be necessary to eliminate weeds.

Characteristics: Chipped bark is becoming increasingly popular. Bark is ground down to produce chips ranging from large 75 x 75mm (3 x 3in) pieces, to a finely chopped mulch. The chips can be used as a ground cover over large areas of planting. The mulch, while ideal as a top-dressing, rots down too quickly for use on paths or play areas; for these, use chips 12–25mm (½–1in) in diameter. Any timber is suitable, but diseased wood should never be used.

Uses: Fine chippings can be used as a water-retentive and weed-suppressing mulch around plants; coarse chippings are best for surfacing paths, steps, ramps, informal sitting areas, and play areas, where they are easy on the knees and overcome the problem of worn grass.

Laying: As a mulch, about 70mm (3in) of finely ground bark should be laid over ground that has been cleaned of perennial weeds. For paths and sitting areas, approximately 25–50mm (1–2in) of coarser bark should be laid over well-compacted soil. Play areas require a thick 70mm (3in) covering of coarse bark laid on geo-textile material over well-consolidated ground. Chippings can usually be allowed to 'drift' into planting alongside; if an edge restraint is necessary or desirable, railway sleepers, logs or boards can be pegged firmly into position.

Contrasting & associating materials: Other timber surfaces, such as railway sleepers, wood slices, log steps, edgings, and decking in informal parts of the garden.

Finely chipped bark provides an ideal mulch both around and below planting. Ample depth is necessary – at least 5–7cm (2–3in) – as the surface will slowly degrade, adding extra organic material to the ground. Topping up is therefore required every two or three years.

PRECAST CONCRETE PAVING

Precast concrete paving is the workhorse of many a hard landscaping scheme and is best used as a simple, no-nonsense background that is suitable for a wide range of activities. Concrete slabs should never be allowed to dominate a scheme. Areas of terracing should be laid to a slight slope to allow water to drain off adequately.

Characteristics: There is a huge range of precast concrete paving available today. Good quality slabs are probably the best and most economical form of reproduction stone paving you can buy, and if laid properly should last a lifetime. They come in many different colours and in a wide variety of textures, so you will need to be strong-minded when choosing. In general, brightly coloured slabs are best avoided; they rarely link with their surroundings, and the colours often fade. Slabs in shades of grey, which blend well with virtually any setting, or those which echo the pale honey-yellow of natural yellow sandstone are by far the best.

Surface textures range from polished aggregate that successfully imitates granite or marble, to coarser, heavily textured aggregates, smooth concrete, or imitation natural stone. Many imitation stone slabs are of poor quality and should be avoided, but some are almost indistinguishable from the real thing – at about half the price. Remember that the more heavily textured the surface, the more uneven it will be for tables and chairs, though it certainly provides excellent grip for paths.

Uses: Paving provides a background to a very wide range of activities, and it is important that the colour and pattern of the slabs do not dominate. It works best with one other surface material; used with brick, for example, an effective visual link can be made with an adjoining building, which will soften the overall effect.

The pattern in which slabs are laid can also play an important role in the overall design. Square slabs laid in a simple grid tend to be static; the same slabs set to a staggered or breaking bond will produce a greater feeling of movement. Rectangular 600 x 300mm (24 x 12in) slabs laid across a space in a staggered bond will draw the space apart and make it feel wider; laid down a terrace or path in this way, they will accelerate the view and possibly foreshorten the space. Random rectangular paving creates the least formal pattern, while paving using broken slabs, will be visually unsettling close to a building, unless contained within a strong framework of another material such as brick or granite setts.

Slabs can also be used for steps, ramps, stepping stones across lawns or through planting, and as broad coping, doubling as occasional seats, on the top of low walls or raised beds.

Laying: As with all paving, correct laying is essential. Bedding slabs on sand is a short-term option that quickly leads to trouble: the surface will become undermined and the slabs uneven. The standard method is to lay a firm base of well-compacted hardcore or crushed stone, and bed the slabs on five spots of mortar – one under each corner and one in the middle. For a driveway, or any area accepting heavy wear, slabs should be bedded on a continuous layer of mortar over a firm base. Any paved area should be set to a slight fall away from the house, or into gullies. Always check the position of drains, manholes or other services, and never pave over or obstruct these.

Slabs can be either butt-jointed as closely together as possible, or laid with a slight gap between them, which is subsequently pointed. The pointing can be flush, rubbed back or raked out; a deep, raked-out joint will create shadow, emphasizing the surface pattern. It is also possible to butt-joint courses of slabs, and rake out the joint to either side. This results in a strong directional emphasis that can be useful in certain design situations.

Stepping stones can be bedded on a weak mortar mix over well-compacted ground, but ensure that the slabs are just below the surface of a lawn, to allow for easy mowing.

Contrasting & associating materials: Nearly all surfaces, hard or soft, because of the range of precast concrete paving available.

Exposed aggregate slabs have an attractive, rugged surface texture that provides both grip and visual interest, and which can often provide an excellent foil to planting. The central joint of this path tends to draw the eye, which has the effect of accelerating the view.

This is an excellent example of a well-made concrete slab that simulates natural stone. The surface is not too heavily textured and the slabs have been perfectly laid. Although this is a random pattern, the courses run across the path, and these, together with the bands of brick, help to widen the space, linking it with the planting on either side.

BRICK

Brick is a warm, mellow and immensely useful paving material that can be laid in a wide range of patterns. Because of its small size, it can be laid to curves and can often be employed to extend a surface into awkward spaces without the need for any cutting.

Characteristics: Brick is one of the finest small modules available for paving; it comes in a vast range of colours, finishes and densities, and can form the perfect link with a house built of the same material. It is important to check with your supplier that what you have chosen will stand up to winter frost; some older bricks break up easily.

Manufacturers are now producing an increasing range of brick 'paviours' specifically for paving. Stable paviours have patterned surfaces, often like that of a bar of chocolate, or impressed with a diamond pattern, and are effective used as a contrast within another surface, or alone for paths or drives where a good grip is important.

Uses: Brick can be used for virtually any kind of paving, but its small size and often dark colour can make it look visually heavy if used alone for large areas. Laying patterns include herringbone (the most complicated), basketweave, stretcher bond and soldier courses; all are more or less demanding on the eye. Once again,

the laying pattern determines the emphasis: where stretcher bond leads the eye on, basketweave produces a more static result.

Laying: All brick paving must be laid over a well-compacted base of hardcore or crushed stone. Bricks can then be bedded on a semi-dry mortar mix, with secure edge restraints at the sides of the path or paved area. Once the pattern has been set out, additional mortar should be carefully brushed into the joints, and the whole area lightly wetted with a fine spray. For a more durable finish, bricks should be bedded into a wet mortar mix, and the joints pointed when it is dry. This must be done with care, as shoddy pointing looks unsightly, and mortar on the face of bricks is extremely difficult to remove. Brick takes longer to lay than, say, natural York stone or precast concrete slabs, and the cost of laying is therefore greater.

Contrasting & associating materials: Brick associates well with virtually all other materials.

LAYING A BRICK PATH
To lay a brick path either bed the bricks in a wet mortar mix, or in a semi-dry mix which is subsequently dampened down. Sound edge restraints are essential.

Brick laid in basketweave pattern

Permanent peg

Timber edging

Mortar

Well-compacted hardcore

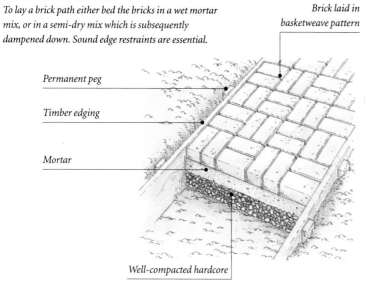

LAYING PATTERNS
Lay bricks either flat, as shown here, or on edge. The latter method obviously uses a greater number of bricks.

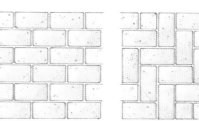  

Stretcher Bond   Herringbone   Basketweave

This herringbone brick floor provides the perfect visual link with the surrounding high brick walls. Such a floor will have a long life if well laid, and its richly textured pattern is the ideal foil for formal planting.

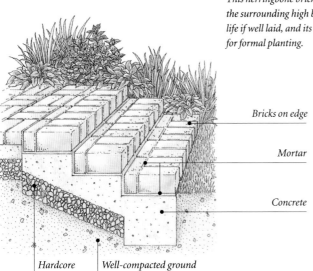

Bricks on edge

Mortar

Concrete

Hardcore   Well-compacted ground

CONSTRUCTING BRICK STEPS
Always build steps to wide, inviting proportions. Sound concrete foundations are a necessity.

As bricks are such small modules, they can be laid to strong flowing curves that lead both feet and eyes through a space. A stretcher bond has the strongest directional emphasis, and here this is reinforced by the dynamic planting to either side of the path.

TILES

Terracotta tiles often have a strong vernacular character that can make them the perfect choice in regional settings. Their mellow colour allows them to blend well with many other hard landscape materials, whether man-made or natural.

Humour is an indispensable part of good garden design and this garden positively oozes both fun and strong character. The deep blue, hand-made tiles link with the coping on the raised beds and pick up the blues of the pot. The arch is bursting with individuality.

LAYING TILES ON EDGE

This is a superb pattern that was traditionally laid using slate rather than tiles. Set all surfaces in mortar over well-consolidated hardcore.

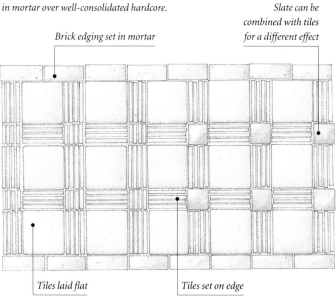

Slate can be combined with tiles for a different effect

Brick edging set in mortar

Tiles laid flat

Tiles set on edge

Characteristics: Like bricks, tiles display a wide regional variation in colour, and not all are frost-proof; this should be checked with the supplier. Terracotta is the most common type and the surface is usually smooth or slightly textured. Sizes are variable from 300mm (12in) square down to 150mm (6in) square. A wide range of patterned glazed tiles is available, but most are too 'busy' for use in the garden.

Uses: Tiles are best suited to smaller, more intimate areas of the garden, where they can be used for paving, steps, or coping on low walls or raised beds. Terracotta tiles can provide a wonderful link with similar tiles inside the house. Roof tiles, like roofing slates, can also be set on edge to produce intricate and elegant paving patterns, a device often used by the architect Sir Edwin Lutyens in the early part of the century.

Laying: Tiles should be bedded in mortar over a base of smooth concrete, and tightly butted together.

Contrasting & associating materials: Tiles are best used on their own but can look effective when carefully integrated with slate or other paving.

CLAY GRANULES

Clay granules provide an excellent mulch in pots or around larger areas of planting. They are particularly useful for use on roof gardens and balconies, where their light weight comes into its own. Their colour blends well with most surfaces, especially terracotta.

Characteristics: Lightweight clay granules, commonly used as a houseplant dressing or growing medium, have a diameter of approximately 6mm (¼in). The brown colour forms a neutral background that blends well with most plants and situations.

Uses: Where weight is an important consideration – on roof gardens, for example – clay granules can be used as a mulch around planting, or as an attractive flooring for parts of the roof that are not walked on, perhaps around a water feature or other focal point. They could be laid in swirling patterns combined with pale-coloured gravel or chippings.

Laying: Tip out of a bag and spread to a depth of about 50mm (2in) over virtually any surface.

Contrasting & associating materials: The neutral colour of the granules blends well with planting and most other hard landscape surfaces.

CONCRETE BLOCKS

Concrete blocks can look much the same as bricks from a distance, but there is less variation in colour which can make large areas of paving appear rather monotonous. This simple stretcher bond leads the eye down the path, reinforcing the line of the low hedges.

Characteristics: Blocks are either approximately the same shape and size as bricks, or are irregular in shape, and interlock to provide added strength. They come in a wide range of colours, including dark grey, red, pink and brown. The surface is clearly concrete but an area paved with these small modules is not unattractive.

Uses: Best suited to driveways and areas of heavy wear. Although cheaper than brick, their rather monotonous colour and surface texture makes them unsuitable for terrace paving or other intimate areas.

Laying: Concrete blocks must be butt-jointed and bedded on sand over a well-consolidated bed of hardcore or crushed stone. Once they are in place, more sand is brushed into the joints and the whole surface compacted with a plate vibrator; this will allow the surface to flex slightly as traffic passes over it. A firm edge restraint is essential. Boards pegged into position are acceptable, but will deteriorate in time; best are special edging blocks set in concrete (available in various patterns to provide differing kerb details). Laying bonds are usually herringbone or basketweave.

Contrasting & associating materials: Usually best on their own, but can be used as panels within a contrasting precast concrete slab.

IN SITU CONCRETE

In situ *concrete can provide a beautifully simple and neutral background on which a wide range of activities can take place. The warm colour shown here is produced by adding a dye to the mix, and links perfectly with the colour scheme used for the adjacent planting.*

Characteristics: *In situ* concrete is laid or cast on site. It can be laid to any shape, which allows great flexibility of design, and the results can be both elegant and cost-effective. Concrete has been called the stone of the twentieth century. Used correctly, with flair and imagination, it is just that, and as its appearance depends on the aggregate (the small stones in the mix) the range of colour and finish is enormous. Surfaces may be smooth, brushed with a broom, seeded with more small stones, exposed by careful washing down and brushing, ribbed, or tamped. Specialist companies will also add dyes to the mix, and impress the surface with patterns to imitate other surfaces. However, these cheap imitations fool no one and are visually dishonest.

Uses: In many different situations, but especially with contemporary designs. It is also useful for free-form shapes where precast concrete slabs would require cutting. The necessity of incorporating expansion joints can become a positive element in the overall design as the surface can be divided by strips of timber, paving slabs, brick or a range of other materials that can in turn be linked back to the house. An excellent, cost-effective choice for drives.

Laying: Must be laid over a well-consolidated base of hardcore or crushed stone. Panels of concrete must be no more than 3.6m (12ft) square, and divided by expansion joints to allow for expansion and contraction at different temperatures. These can be formed of strips of timber, paving slabs, brick, or any of a wide range of other materials.

LAYING IN SITU *CONCRETE*

In situ *concrete can be cast to virtually any pattern with a wide range of aggregate or other finishes.*

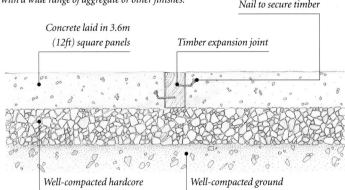

Nail to secure timber

Concrete laid in 3.6m (12ft) square panels

Timber expansion joint

Well-compacted hardcore

Well-compacted ground

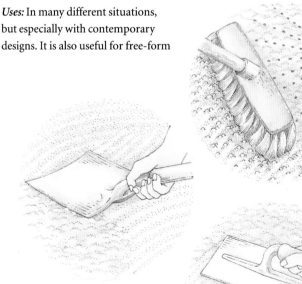

ACHIEVING DIFFERENT FINISHES
Several different finishes are possible, including smoothing with a shovel for a slightly textured finish, brushing with a broom to expose the aggregate in the mix, or using a steel float for a smooth finish.

These no-nonsense concrete steps are both well-proportioned and well-constructed, linking with the concrete balustrade that borders the flight. Architectural planting plays an important role in softening the inevitable hard lines, while shadows add visual drama.

An edge restraint is only necessary while laying and this can be used to make part of the overall pattern of expansion joints. If timber boards are used these can be struck (removed) once the surface has dried out. The concrete itself should be approximately 70mm (3in) thick, and if an exposed aggregate finish is required, the stones chosen must be added to the ballast before the concrete is mixed. Other finishes can be implemented as the concrete is laid or drying out. In hot weather cover the surface with damp sacking or burlap to prevent it from drying out too quickly; if there is any danger of frost, it should be covered with plastic sheeting until completely dry.

Contrasting & associating materials: Best with other man-made materials, but some natural materials provide a good contrast for expansion joints.

PLASTICS

Astroturf is best thought of as carpet rather than imitation grass. It provides an ideal floor in many situations, particularly roof gardens or around swimming pools. There is too much horticultural snobbery surrounding such surfaces, use them for what they are!

Characteristics: Plastics have a great deal to offer. Plastic turf, known as Astroturf, is commonly used for sports fields; it is also useful on roof gardens or around swimming pools. It is light, durable, and comes in brown and black as well as green. Other industrial and sports arena floorings are also available; they, too, are extremely durable, and come in a varied range of exciting colours and textures.

Uses: Plastic and other synthetic floorings can be used in any part of the garden, but are especially useful on roof gardens because of their light weight. They are particularly suited to contemporary, hi-tech settings. The large, flexible sheets can be cut to form strong, flowing curves, providing great fluidity in a design, and can be moulded over ramps, eliminating the need for steps in certain situations. The possibilities of mixing and matching swirls of colour, both outdoors and in, are exciting and limitless!

Laying: Plastic flooring must be laid, like vinyl flooring in the home, on a screed over a sound concrete base. It can sometimes be laid over existing paving. Whereas industrial flooring often needs to be fixed down with adhesive, Astroturf can simply be rolled out and cut to fit.

Contrasting & associating materials: Plastic and other synthetic flooring is best used on its own and usually works in a contemporary setting; it does not associate very happily with other hard landscape materials.

TRIMS & EDGES

Trims can play an important role in terms of design, and here the box hedge provides vertical emphasis while the polished slate stones beneath provide definition at a lower level. Neither of these elements gives a great degree of physical containment.

Good hard landscaping is all about attention to detail, and one of the most important details is how to finish or retain surfacing materials. However, following the classic design rule of simplicity, edging should only be used if the surface actually needs it. You will often see an area of precast concrete slabs or brick paving edged with a concrete kerb, a row of granite setts or cast rope edging. They are unnecessary and look fussy.

Surfaces which do need an edge or trim are usually 'fluid' – either permanently (e.g. gravel or wood chips) or temporarily until they set (e.g. *in situ* concrete or asphalt).

Some, such as concrete blocks, need an edge restraint to prevent the surface moving outwards and losing its integrity. Occasionally a trim can be used as a contrast to the main surface (e.g. natural paving or precast concrete slabs edging a gravel or cobble path), but this must be an integral part of the design and not design for design's sake! Trims can also be invaluable as a mowing edge.

Many surfacing materials can be used as edges and trims: brick, granite setts, timber, and precast concrete slabs among them. Always suit the edging to the surface material and to the situation. A curving path

or driveway is best edged with small modules such as bricks or setts that will conform to the shape. Longer lengths of inflexible materials will form a visually uncomfortable edge.

Any form of edge must be securely fixed in position, either haunched in concrete, or, for timber, pegged into position, before the surface area is laid. Haunching consists of setting the edging in a concrete foundation that is chamfered away on the outside, allowing it to be covered with and hidden by soil, planting or grass. In the case of a mowing edge, slabs or bricks should be set in mortar or concrete just below the level of the turf. Although trims and edgings form only a small part of the cost of the surface you choose, check the details against the information provided for individual materials.

Brick: Bricks are immensely versatile and can be used with a wide range of surfaces. They are best laid on edge, either end to end, or side by side, which uses more bricks but looks more stable. The small brick modules allow straight or curved runs to be catered for, as well as surrounds for trees or planting. They also make an ideal mowing edge.

Concrete kerb edgings: These are cheap and much loved by builders. Unfortunately they look it! Approximately 900mm (36in) long and 230mm (9in) deep, they should be used only as a last resort, and then only for straight runs.

Granite setts: One of the most useful trims. Full or half setts can be used to edge gravel, chippings, brushed

aggregate, concrete or lawns. They will conform easily to curves, and can be used in a single, double, or treble row for greater visual emphasis. They can also be used within a gravel or hoggin area to form a surround to trees or other planting. Setts should be haunched in concrete.

Metal strips: Used in many established and historic gardens. Wrought iron or steel edging strips provide crisp, no-nonsense trims that can look superb, particularly when retaining a slightly higher lawn at the edge of a drive. They can be used for straight or curved runs. These trims will last virtually for ever, but are expensive, often difficult to obtain, and their installation is a specialist job. Never confuse them with the flimsy corrugated alloy edging that can be bought in rolls from garden centres. This is barely strong enough to retain anything, will eventually get mangled in the mower (doing neither of them any good), and should be avoided at all cost.

Precast concrete slabs: These can make a well-detailed edge for a wide range of materials, including gravel, hoggin, brushed aggregate or cobbles. The width and colour of the slabs should be chosen to fit in with the overall design of the garden. They are best for straight runs; slabs designed for curves should be avoided like the plague as they only exist in set sizes and look terrible.

Rope edgings: Ever popular, these are available in cast concrete (which can look untidy), terracotta, or stone. They look decidedly uncomfortable

Granite setts form a simple, no-nonsense and firm trim to many surfaces: in this case, an asphalt path. Planting can be allowed to flop over and soften the hard edges.

These traditional clay Victorian or Edwardian edgings are full of character, showing the patina and irregularities of age. Frost-proof engineering bricks act as a mowing edge.

Glazed terracotta 'rope' edgings are both elegant and durable – they should last for well over a hundred years – and they can form an ideal restraint for gravel paths.

WOODEN EDGING FOR A GRAVEL PATH
This pressure-treated timber edge will have a long life, notice how the top of the stake is chamfered, making it virtually invisible.

Gravel · Pressure-treated board · Hoggin · Well-compacted hardcore · Pressure-treated wooden peg

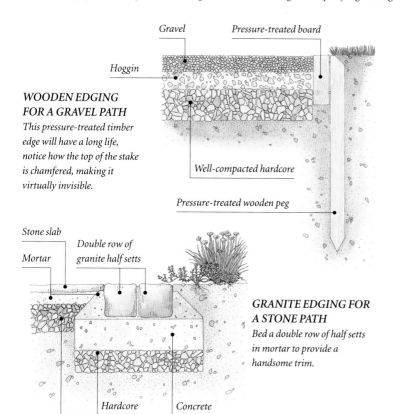

Stone slab · Mortar · Double row of granite half setts · Hardcore · Concrete

GRANITE EDGING FOR A STONE PATH
Bed a double row of half setts in mortar to provide a handsome trim.

in a contemporary setting, and are best used as a trim for a gravel or hoggin path. They should be firmly set in concrete to prevent movement.

Tiles: Laid side by side with just the edge visible, these form a delicate and intricate trim that can look superb in the right place. This effect requires a large number of frost-proof tiles, which should be set in mortar over a concrete foundation.

Timber: Boards, approximately 150 x 18mm (6 x ¾in), are the most cost-effective, and since they are flexible can be used to edge both straight and curved paths. Boards should be pressure-treated and pegged into position on the outside. Pegs 450mm (18in) long are hammered into the ground to just below the top of the boards, and the boards nailed to them.

Round sawn logs make an attractive informal edging, either placed in a trench and held in position with rammed soil, or set in concrete. They will easily conform to a curve. Unsawn logs make the most informal edging of all, and are perfect for a wood chip or rough grass path through woodland. Heavy logs can simply be placed and left in position. Railway sleepers make a powerful edge for gravel, hoggin, cobbles or wood chips, but are only suitable for straight runs. Thanks to their weight, they can be laid simply on sifted soil over well-compacted ground.

Natural stone: A superb, traditional edging for straight cobbled or gravelled paths. Strips approximately 300mm (12in) wide are set on edge, butt-jointed, and set in concrete to make a handsome mowing edge.

LAWNS

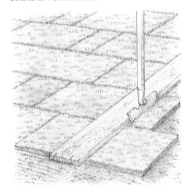

For a straight edge, cut along the edge of a board using a half-moon edger.

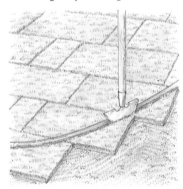

Set out curves from a predetermined radius point and mark with a hose or line, prior to cutting through the turf.

The design permutations for using grass are virtually endless. In this strongly geometric pattern the whole area dishes down towards the level central circle. The octagonal gravel paths and surrounding hedges emphasize the underlying shape, the latter providing screening and shelter at the highest level.

The greater part of your garden floor may well be given over to soft landscape in the form of grass, ground cover or planting. The planting is outside the scope of this book, but grass and ground cover are very much part of the overall design and organization of space.

Chamomile, thyme and other ground-hugging plants can also be used as lawns, but good, old-fashioned grass is still the most valuable and cost-effective flooring available in the garden. It is tough, easy to lay, straightforward to maintain, and remains the most suitable surface for the widest possible range of activities. It also looks good, especially in a temperate climate, where it will thrive in the moist conditions. The kind of lawn you choose will depend on the appearance

you wish it to have, and the amount of maintenance you are prepared to undertake.

Grass lawns can be either seeded or turfed. In general, a turfed lawn will establish more quickly than a seeded one, and the preparations for a seeded lawn are rather more critical. The quality of either will be determined by the type of seed mix. A lawn with a hard-wearing surface that will cope with the demands of children, dogs, sporting grown-ups, and social life, will need a relatively high percentage of tough, broad-leafed species of grass. That epitome of the English garden, on the other hand, the perfect 'bowling green' lawn with its immaculate cylinder mower stripes, is made up from finer grasses. Such stripes have a powerful visual effect in a design. If a long, narrow lawn is

mown up and down its length, the shape is emphasized. Try mowing it across, or diagonally, to increase the visual width. The air of mystery that is achieved by a lawn disappearing around a curve or wing of planting, can be reinforced by a mowing pattern that follows the shape of the lawn, producing a sense of space and movement.

Weeding, feeding and cherishing a lawn does undoubtedly improve it, but weed seed, especially in country areas, will continue to invade, and it may be wiser to tolerate a degree of weeds and tough grasses for the sake of a surface that will wear better and be easier to maintain. Avoid, too, cutting your grass too short, which inhibits growth and allows the lawn to dry out in hot weather; 12–25mm (½–1in) is ideal.

The combination of rough grass and wild flowers is simply delightful. To look at its best, however, a composition like this needs to be sited in an area that is large enough to allow the paths to curve away out of sight into the background.

Other elements also affect ease of maintenance. Complicated patterns of lawn make mowing difficult, and hand edging is a chore. So work out a bold and simple ground plan that links with the rest of the garden pattern, and lay a mowing edge of brick or slabs that will allow the mower to run smoothly over the top, eliminating the need for hand edging and protecting plants.

Areas of rough grass: As a general rule, the further away from the house, the softer and looser the composition can become. Shorn sward can give way to rougher grass that will look ideal beneath fruit trees, and a path mown through rough grass is always a delight. Such an area can be naturalized with bulbs and even wild flowers – although wild flowers thrive in relatively lean conditions, and rich, fertile garden soil may well encourage

stronger grasses and perennial weeds at their expense. Do not be disheartened if your display does not quite match that of the wild flower lawns at horticultural shows! Grass like this needs cutting only three times a year: once after the spring bulbs have died down, once after the summer flowers have set seed, and once before putting the area to bed for the winter.

Alpines: Many of the mat-forming alpine plants can be used as charming carpeters in areas that are not much walked on. They can be grown in cracks between paving, helping to soften the overall surface, or as a larger carpet, when sweeps of several different species can swirl and intertwine, setting up a delightful dialogue. Nearly all alpines need a free-draining gritty soil and plenty of sun if they are to thrive.

Chamomile: Chamomile lawns have a long history, they don't need cutting and are wonderfully fragrant when trodden on. To cross a chamomile lawn and sit enjoying the scent on a fine summer's evening is one of the great pleasures of life. They are fine in formal areas where traffic is light, but they do take a long time

to establish, need constant weeding while establishing, and cannot tolerate heavy wear. The variety to plant is the non-flowering cultivar, *Chamaemelum nobile* 'Treneague'.

Soleirolia: *S. soleirolii* (syn. *Helxine soleirolii*) or 'mind your own business' is a tiny-leafed plant, often considered a rampant weed. As a filler in cracks between paving, or as a ground cover, it forms a dense green mat of superb foliage, thriving in shade and impossible conditions. It will not survive heavy wear, and should be kept well away (if possible) from other planting or conventional lawns.

Thyme: Like chamomile, thyme will not tolerate heavy wear, and takes a while to establish. However, its natural ground-hugging character makes it an ideal carpeter, and the bonus of flower is a real one. Grow *Thymus serpyllum* and *T. doerfleri*, both deliciously fragrant when crushed underfoot. Or, use them for a thyme seat or a thyme table, growing the plants in a reasonably deep tray and remembering to water them. The effect will be worth the effort, and will always provide a talking point.

Chamomile is a naturally ground hugging species that quickly forms a fragrant carpet, although it will only be able to survive light wear. In this imaginative design, the rope pattern, set within the brick paving, has enormous movement which is reinforced by the equally fragrant lavender planted on either side.

GROUND COVER

Many plants, too tall to be in the category of lawns, can still be used to form a horizontal carpet for the garden. These ground-cover plants will exclude weed growth, and can be used to reinforce the floor pattern while keeping maintenance to a minimum. There are many suitable species, but you will need to do your homework to check the soil type and aspect that they prefer, as well as their height and spread. Plant labels will often give you the information you need. Resist the temptation to overplant; many ground covers are rampant and knit together fast. As with any planting, sound preparation is the secret of success. Make sure that the soil is well cultivated, free from perennial weeds, and contains as much organic matter as possible.

The following is not a comprehensive catalogue, simply a selection of available plants.

Ajuga reptans: There are a number of different bugles; 'Atropurpurea' is one of the best. Suitable for sun or part shade, all are ground-hugging and not too invasive.

Bergenia: Large, rounded evergreen leaves, and pink or white flowers in spring. Excellent ground cover for sun or shade, and tolerant of a wide range of soils. *B. cordifolia* and its cultivars are the most suitable.

Cistus x *dansereaui* 'Decumbens' (syn. *C.* x *lusitanicus* 'Decumbens')*:* A wide-spreading, evergreen rock rose, ideal in full sun. The delicate white flowers are patterned with a crimson blotch at the centre.

Cotoneaster x *suecicus* 'Skogholm'*:* Low, ground-hugging, excellent in sun or partial shade. Bears a profusion of red berries in the autumn.

Epimedium: Neat, low grower with small, heart-shaped leaves and delicate pink, white or yellow flowers on wiry stems. This is ideal in shade, and although it is reasonably quick to establish, it should not be too invasive.

Low-growing ground covers, for example moss and Soleirolia, are ideal in damp, shady conditions, such as those found beneath trees. They need little attention, apart from keeping them moist in dry weather. In this situation, the visual dialogue with the loose cobbles is an interesting one, both surfaces producing complete carpets.

Euphorbia: Many of the lower-growing spurges make good ground cover. *E. polychroma* is deciduous; *E. amygdaloïdes* var. *robbiae* semi-evergreen. Both have lime-green flower heads, and both are best in sun or partial shade.

Geranium: There are many herbaceous geraniums or cranesbills, varying in colour of flower, and in height from 60–90cm (24–36in) to semi-prostrate. The majority make superb ground cover and most like sun, though *G. endressii* thrives in shaded, open areas.

Hebe pinguifolia 'Pagei'*:* A fine, low-growing, ground-covering hebe, with white flowers and glaucous-grey foliage. This does well in sun, and I have it thriving in light shade.

Hedera: Nearly all the ivies make terrific ground cover, and are one of the best plants to choose for shaded areas. They have the added advantage of being capable of running up any vertical surface that gets in their way. Most are fast-growing and invasive. There is a wide range of leaf shape, size, colour and variegation to choose from.

Hosta: No garden is complete without hostas. They thrive in sun or shade, have a vast range of leaf colour, and knit together without being rampant. All are deciduous.

Hypericum calycinum: Perhaps the best known of all ground covers, the rose of Sharon displays both the advantages and disadvantages of this group. This low-growing evergreen carries yellow buttercup flowers throughout the summer, and enjoys sun or shade. It is extremely invasive and needs to be confined, or rapidly cut back should it invade other areas.

Lamium: The much maligned 'dead nettle' makes an excellent choice in full or partial shade. Strong-growing, and therefore best where it can be contained, it is ideal under trees. *L. maculatum* 'Beacon Silver' is one of the best.

Lonicera pileata: Low-growing evergreen ground cover with arching, horizontal branches. Good in sun or shade, with bright green spring foliage. Small, white flowers in spring are followed by unusual translucent violet berries.

Nepeta: Catmint or catnip, is one of the most useful ground covers in full sun and well-drained soils. I like to grow it under roses, which is sacrilege to the purists but looks great.

Pachysandra terminalis: Evergreen, suitable for deep shade, with white flowers. Relatively slow to establish, it enjoys acid soil. There is also a useful variegated form.

Polygonatum: Solomon's seal is excellent in shade and in deep, rich, damp soils. The greenish-white bell-shaped flowers appear in late spring.

Pulmonaria: *P. saccharata* is the lungwort most commonly grown, and it does well in full or partial shade, preferring a moist but not waterlogged soil. Attractively blotchy leaves, and pink and blue flowers in spring.

Stachys byzantina: Lamb's lugs or lamb's ears, with their soft, felty grey leaves, are excellent in full sun and poor soils. The cultivar 'Silver Carpet' is especially good as ground cover.

Symphoricarpos x *chenaultii* 'Hancock':
Provides good ground cover for both sun and shade, even when planted beneath trees. The white flowers are insignificant, but the whitish pink berries that appear in autumn continue well into winter.

Symphytum grandiflorum: Good, spreading ground cover beneath trees in moist, cool soil. Flowers for a long period in spring, with creamy tube-like flowers.

Vinca minor: The periwinkle is an invasive evergreen, happy in sun or shade, with blue flowers borne over a long period. There is a variegated form, and a variety with larger flowers, *V. major.*

Ivy is available in a vast range of variegations and leaf shapes. I favour the simpler green varieties – the risers of these steps are transformed by such planting.

This is the perfect marriage of hard and soft landscaping, the slabs forming an abstract chequerboard pattern that is softened by the luxuriant carpet of moss. A rampant ground cover such as this should either be contained or, if space permits, allowed to drift off into an informal area where it can fade out without being too invasive.

45

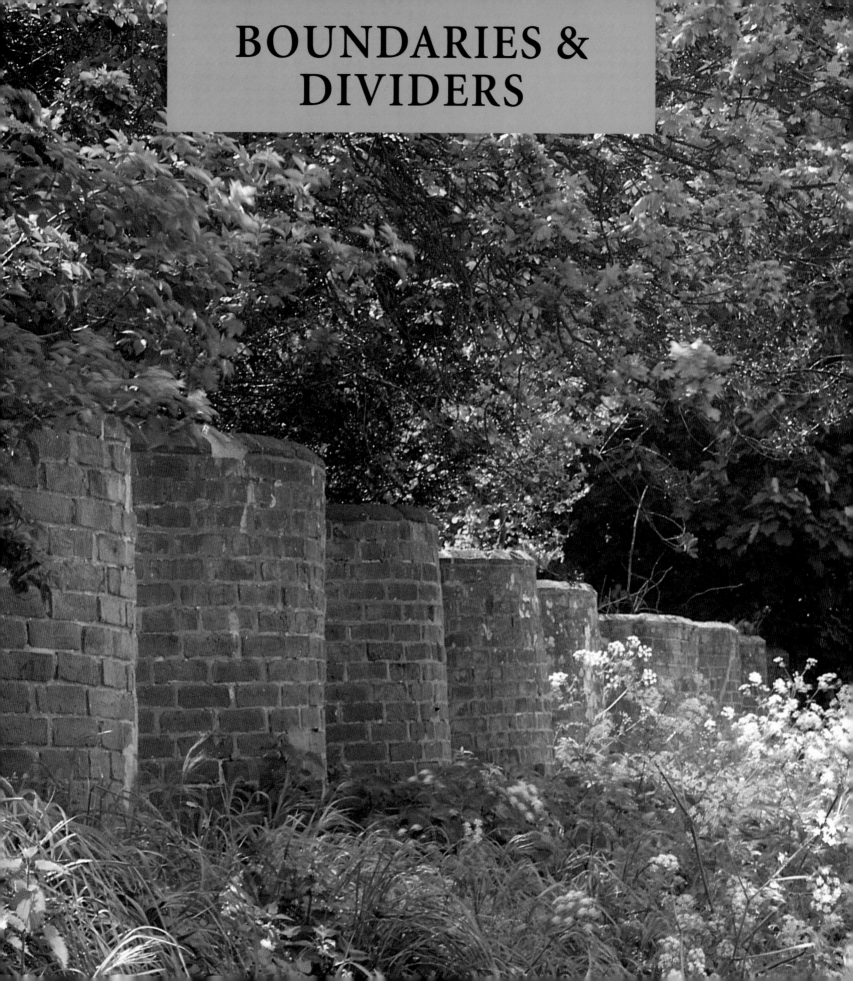

BOUNDARIES &
DIVIDERS

Above: *Boundary treatments are infinitely variable and this is a fascinating contrast in materials and form. The solidity of the piers is all the more telling in their juxtaposition with the simple timber rails and the vertical palings in the background.*

Opposite: *Dividers not only separate different areas of the garden but also contain individual spaces at the same time. Where a screen is pierced, plants can be allowed to grow through: here the fence rises through green clouds of Alchemilla mollis.*

Like the inside of a house, a garden will have finite boundaries, and may also have internal divisions enclosing different areas. Whether these divisions are purely practical, are designed to screen specific utility areas, or are of a more decorative nature, used to provide a feeling of tension, mystery and surprise, will depend on the site and the overall design of the garden.

Boundaries

The prime object of a boundary is to define the garden perimeter. It may also, but not always, provide privacy, afford protection and shelter from wind or noise, and keep people or animals inside or outside the space.

A garden where privacy is important, where children need to be secure, and which is subject to a strong prevailing wind, would almost certainly need a solid boundary of some kind – possibly reinforced with planting to act as a filter for the wind. A garden in the country, on the other hand, with fine views and adequate shelter from the

wind and passing traffic, might only need an open post and rail fence, iron park fencing, or even a sunken barrier such as a ha-ha.

Practical considerations apart, there may be aesthetic reasons for choosing a particular type of boundary. A brick or stone wall, for example, could make a natural extension from a building of the same material, thus providing a strong link between house and garden. Since there is probably a public as well as a private face to your boundary, there is also a certain moral obligation to choose one that will blend with its surroundings, especially where there is a strong local identity.

Hard boundaries may also be constructed from more than one material; this mix and match approach can be both elegant and attractive. The rules, however, remain the same: two different materials are probably enough; too many form a visually busy effect that is counter-productive. Sometimes materials can be mixed within the same run: a brick wall with panels of broken flint, for example; or well-detailed stone piers with trellis or panel inserts. In another situation, an existing low wall may need raising to increase privacy; here, carefully constructed trellis could be used in conjunction with planting.

Cost, of course, is important, and since the boundary may well take the lion's share of your garden budget, it makes sense to consider the alternatives with care. Walls are expensive, post and wire fences far cheaper; but the equation should include the job the boundary is required to do, its durability, and its maintenance requirements. For many of us, a fence will provide the most practical and cost-effective solution, and this will often take the form of a timber panel or board fence. Either can be perfectly satisfactory, and provide an opportunity for originality and innovation. It is just a pity that manufacturers on the one hand, and erectors on the other, use them with so little imagination or respect for detail.

Hedges will often provide virtually the same results as a fabricated boundary at a fraction of the cost. A well-grown and well-clipped hedge is hard to beat, and will form a wonderful backdrop for planting. Hedges make far better windbreaks than walls or fences (which tend to create their own turbulence on the lee side), by filtering rather than stopping the wind. They can also help to muffle the noise of traffic, and reduce traffic pollution. On the debit side, they take time to establish, and will need regular maintenance in the form of clipping and feeding. It may also be necessary to erect a temporary fence until the hedge is established.

The plant species chosen will affect the character of the garden, and will influence planting, the positioning of features, and the way space and views are handled. The rich, dark evergreen of clipped yew will always give an air of formality to a garden, while an informal hedge of locally found species can be used to blend comfortably into the landscape.

Gates and entrances are important features, and it is surprising how often they are simply slotted into a boundary with no real thought. The Victorians were consummate gate-makers, and their good designs and well-built examples can still be seen outside many an old rectory or domestic house.

The paramount rule when selecting or designing a gate is that it should be in harmony with the rest of the fence, wall, or divider. As a general rule, it should respect the height of the adjoining boundary, though with a low fence it is sometimes attractive to take the gate higher, perhaps within an arch. This will form a real punctuation point that will draw both feet and eye towards it.

Screens and dividers

A garden that can be seen at one glance is usually far less interesting than one that is divided into separate rooms, each with a different theme, colour scheme or purpose. The divisions can be achieved in many different ways; as for boundaries, walls, fences and hedges can be used, but so, too, can more open frameworks which allow a partial view through.

Well-positioned dividers can, as we know, create a feeling of mystery, tension and surprise. We never fail to be attracted by the mystery of what lies beyond a wing of trellis, a honeycomb brick wall, or a hedge; there is a feeling of tension and expectancy as we approach, which is released by the surprise of discovery as we enter. Such devices are called 'tension points' by professionals, and are one of the most useful tools at the designer's disposal.

Slavishly following fashion can be a dangerous thing, especially as the same trends tend to come around on a cyclical basis. Trellis, for instance, is once again extremely popular and much used as a divider. It is also used for garden features, supports for plants, and to raise the level of boundary walls. On the positive side, this means that a lot of thought has gone into reviving the best old designs and creating new ones. On the down side, trendy manufacturers, garden designers and gardeners still love those impossibly convoluted designs revealed in Victorian and Edwardian gardening books, and with this kind of *treillage* it is all too easy to fall into the trap of overcomplication. The material available is also often of poor quality, and even more often, inappropriately used. There is nothing worse than using trellis for trellis's sake. However, if it is well made, well designed, and well used, good quality trellis can play an important part in the overall design of the garden.

Dividers do not have to be higher than eye-level, and a space can be effectively punctuated by hedges or parterres at a much lower level. Taken to extremes, a garden can even be visually divided by the subtle use of light and shadow; a tree or high wall can cast a band of shade across an area with dramatic effect, even in the soft light of a temperate climate.

Avenues, too, can be used to divide space in a dramatic way, whether on a grand scale with substantial trees flanking a drive to a fine country house, or in a more intimate way, taking the form of clipped shrubs or even a row of well-planted pots on either side of a path.

Whatever material we eventually decide upon, dividing a space effectively depends, like so many of the designer's 'tricks of the trade', on commonsense, an appreciation of scale, the use of form and, not least, sensible positioning!

DRY STONE WALLS

This dramatic and beautiful dry stone wall uses a wide range of materials to form a composition that is more a work of art than a standard boundary treatment. The planting at a higher level provides an effective counterpoint to the delicate stonework.

BUILDING A DRY STONE WALL

Set a dry stone wall over a foundation of large stones before building the wall to a taper or 'batter' which will help to provide extra stability.

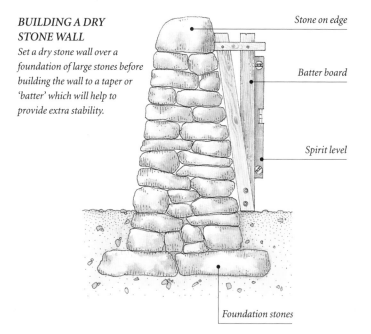

Stone on edge

Batter board

Spirit level

Foundation stones

Characteristics: Dry stone walls were originally used as field boundaries, and have a strongly regional and rural character. This makes them look totally comfortable in an area where such stone is found naturally, and outrageously pretentious elsewhere. They are commonly found in many parts of the British Isles, and in rural areas throughout the world.

The quality and colour of stone varies enormously: grit, limestone, sandstone, granite, slate may all show subtle variations within the space of a few miles. The character of the walls is also affected by the natural irregularity of the stones, which are often simply gathered from the surrounding land. Even when perfectly laid, the faces will have rich textures and shadows, and pockets of soil will allow sprawling plants to be introduced, reinforcing the informal effect. Flatter, less rounded stones are normally selected as these provide the greatest stability. Because no mortar is used, dry stone walls should never be built to more than waist-height, and while this will provide a physical boundary, it will not ensure privacy.

Uses: Dry stone walls translate happily into a village environment, but look distinctly out of place in the more formal character of a town. They look perfectly at home surrounding a field or a large country garden. They also look comfortable framing a much smaller space where the house, too, is built of stone, and will provide a natural link between the two. They should not be used for load-bearing or for more substantial

constructions, but are excellent for raised beds, dividers, and low retaining walls.

Construction: This is a skilled job, best undertaken by local craftsmen, with much of the skill lying in the selection of stones during construction. Foundations are usually minimal and simply consist of large slabs of stone laid well beneath ground level. The wall is built in two halves, with the centre packed with rubble. Larger stones are used at the bottom, and smaller at the top, to ensure that both faces are angled slightly inward towards the top. Some craftsmen use a spirit- or carpenters' level placed against a special wooden template to ensure that this 'batter' is correctly aligned.

Walls can be regularly or randomly coursed, depending very much on the shape of the stone, and are reinforced by the addition of through stones running from one side to the other, as work progresses. Gaps between stones are wedged with slivers of rock. Coping often takes the form of stones set on edge; where these are alternately higher or lower, they are known as 'cocks and hens'.

Dry stone walls should always follow the lie of the land, and should never be stepped up or down.

Contrasting & associating materials: Dry stone walling associates naturally with gravel and stone paving. It also looks particularly handsome with timber, in the form of well-detailed fencing, railway sleepers or decking. Decking positioned close to dry stone walling can look effective when used in a contemporary cottage garden.

This wall displays craftsmanship at its very best, and has been built in courses using carefully selected stones of roughly similar thickness but different lengths. Additional character, colour and texture are provided by the lichens that have colonized the wall face.

STONE HEDGES & TURF BANKS

Stone banks have a deliciously rural feel, and will only look comfortable if they are constructed in an area with appropriate surroundings. Plants will readily colonize, but you can give them a helping hand by scooping out pockets and introducing material artificially.

Characteristics: Stone hedges and turf banks are strongly regional, rural boundary treatments that look best in their own locality. They are predominantly found in the west of England and in certain other parts of the world. Both have a core of rammed soil, so the overall width is relatively great, and they are rarely built over chest height.

Uses: Both can be used to provide a subtle link between garden and landscape, with plants introduced, or allowed to self-seed, on their face. They are totally stock-proof and can make a superb boundary for a large country garden adjoining farmland or paddocks, but their bulk makes them unsuitable for small spaces.

Construction: Skilled and practised craftsmen are essential, and it is a sad fact that these are becoming harder to find. Both stone hedges and turf banks are built with a pronounced batter, and turf banks especially are considerably wider at the bottom than the top. Stone banks are built in a similar way to dry stone walls, but with soil used between the stones. The core in each case is made from a mixture of stone and rammed soil, the soil usually being taken from one side to form a ditch. Turf banks are then covered with sods held in position with wooden pegs until they take hold, and stone hedges are faced with stones of varying size.

Contrasting & associating materials: Such a strong feature needs a strong use of materials around it. Natural stone paving, gravel, chippings and timber in the form of railway sleepers or logs all associate well.

MORTARED STONE WALLS

Mortared stone walls can last a very long time and often provide an ideal host to all kinds of planting. This example shows a particularly good method of dealing with a gateway, the line of the wall has been gently swept over the top of the gate in a rhythmical curve.

Characteristics: A well-built and carefully pointed mortared stone wall will have the same characteristics as a dry stone wall, and like it, will look best in regions where stone occurs naturally. Aesthetic considerations will be the same. The difference is that a mortared wall is considerably stronger and can therefore be built to a greater height.

Uses: Since mortared stone walls can be built to about 1.8m (6ft) in height, they can be used where privacy is important. They can also be used for load-bearing, or as retaining walls – either on their own or as facing for brick or concrete blocks.

Construction: Unlike dry stone walls, mortared stone walls can be built by any competent bricklayer. Methods vary in different areas, and it is important to look around for good examples, and appreciate the skills involved. Concrete footings should suit the ground conditions, and be about twice as wide as the 450mm (18in) base of the wall. Like a dry stone wall, the mortared wall is built in two halves, with a core of rubble running through the centre, but usually without through stones. It can either be built to a batter, or vertical, and will look best if it is

coursed. Courses can be made up of different-sized stones – one course of 70mm (3in) stones; one of 150mm (6in) stones; a third of 100mm (4in) stones, for example. Occasional jumpers (larger stones that span two courses) can be inserted as work progresses.

Careful pointing is essential. This can either be raked back to create shadows that will emphasize the strongly textured face, or neatly rubbed to provide a softer, indented joint. Mortar that is squashed out of the joints like toothpaste simply degrades the stone.

Coping can be the traditional stone on edge, a rounded fillet of mortar, or even brick on edge. My own house is built of pale Northampton stone, and I have constructed walls of the same material. The coping consists of a double row of blue bull-nosed engineering brick, which matches the slate roof of the house and contrasts beautifully with the stone.

Contrasting & associating materials: Natural stone paving, gravel or chippings. Solid timberwork such as railway sleepers or decking. Sections of slatted timber fence can also look handsome if the overall run is carefully integrated.

BUILDING A MORTARED STONE WALL

Like unmortared walls, these gain added strength if they are built to a batter. Use raked or rubbed back joints for the pointing.

Flat stones as coping

Mortared joints

Concrete footings

STONE BLOCKS

This generous arch has enormous visual power and is built from large pieces of dressed stone, softened by the overhanging fronds of ivy. The theme is continued at ground level where the stonework of the arch is reflected in the intricately worked pattern of setts.

Characteristics: Sawn, or dressed, stone is the king of walling, but this beautiful material is so expensive that it is only really viable for very high-cost projects. Like all natural stone, it has enormous colour and textural variations, depending on its source, and the smooth face will also be dressed with different textures; pouncing (an indented finish) is popular in certain parts of the country. Blocks are usually regular in size, which helps to create a crisp, architectural pattern. Joints are pointed with mortar to match the stone; these are either left flush, or carefully raked back to provide well-defined shadow lines.

Uses: Walls made of sawn stone are traditionally used for fine houses and adjoining boundaries in both town and country, but they can be used to devastating effect with both traditional and contemporary architecture. They are perfect in areas where the stone is quarried. In a garden setting, stone can be used as a frame and teamed with brick. Stone walls topped with wrought-iron railings are exceptionally elegant, though horrendously expensive.

Construction: This is firmly in the realm of the stonemason; if you can afford the stone, you can also afford the professionals to put it up! Solid concrete foundations are essential, and the mortar should contain stone dust so that it matches exactly. Coping is usually made from natural stone, often carefully shaped to a traditional profile.

Contrasting & associating materials: Stone walls and gravel drives are quite simply close to God. They look good, too. Elegant planting schemes of hardy perennials, sweeping English lawns and a carefully parked Aston Martin DB5 complete the picture – dream on!

HA-HAS

New ha-has are expensive to build, but in the right setting, they can be well worth the price. Attention to detail is always important, and the vernacular construction of brick and flint in this contemporary example matches the materials used in the nearby house.

Characteristics: Ha-has were one of the great landscape devices of the eighteenth century. They consisted of a sunken ditch, faced on the house side with a retaining wall and often with a fence at the bottom, that allowed a view to run smoothly out into the surrounding parkland, while preventing cattle or other livestock from getting in. The object was to provide an apparently seamless transition from the grass in front of the house into the landscape beyond, and the spoil from the ditch was often used to create a smooth ramp up to the ha-ha from the house, which augmented the effect still further.

Uses: Ha-has are still built today, and if the budget will stand the cost, make a far better boundary than the over-used and obtrusive post and rail fence. The line of the ha-ha can be continued with a fence, once the boundary is hidden from the house or main viewpoint.

Construction: Ha-has require a great deal of excavation. In a parkland setting, the distance from one end to the other may be considerable, and the ditch itself will be at least 1.8m (6ft) deep, with a retaining wall of the same height. The wall may be built of concrete blocks but is usually faced in brick, brick and flint, or stone, depending on the local material, and angled into the bank to form a slight batter. The installation of land drains may be necessary to prevent the ditch becoming a moat.

Contrasting & associating materials: Not applicable.

BRICK WALLS

This is a perfect example of hard landscape at its best. Old brick has a mellow character that can often compensate for slight irregularities in construction. The steps, with tile risers that match the colour of the brick, and punctuated by delicate star-like daisies, effectively extend the line of the wall out into the garden.

Characteristics: One of the oldest constructional materials known to man, brick is produced today in much the same way as it was thousands of years ago. It confirms the old adage that the simplest things work best: bricks are simply rectangular blocks of burnt clay; easy to make, easy to lay, and exceptionally durable. Brick is also beautiful, showing huge variations in colour and texture – variations that depend on the local clay and the length of firing time in the kiln. If you cross any country that produces brick, you will notice these local variations, especially in the vernacular architecture; it was not so long ago that every town and village had its own brickworks, producing bricks that looked comfortably at home in the built environment.

The same is true of garden walls. You will see both fine old walls and new ones that extend the line and character of a building into the wider landscape or townscape. They provide a cue to the use of a similar brick within the garden, either as dividers or floors.

DOUBLE THICKNESS BRICK WALL

Always build foundations to twice the width of the wall and deep enough to suit your soil conditions. Insert pegs at regular intervals and to the same height, then bring the concrete up to the tops of the pegs. Flemish bond has been used here, with a radiused brick coping.

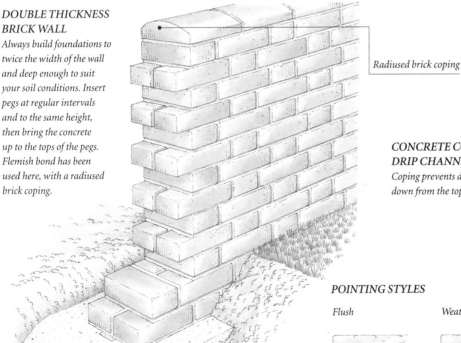

Radiused brick coping

Level pegs for foundation　　*Concrete foundation*

CONCRETE COPING WITH DRIP CHANNELS

Coping prevents dampness percolating down from the top of the wall.

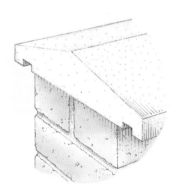

POINTING STYLES

Flush　　*Weathered*　　*Rubbed back*

Pointing prevents dampness penetrating the joints of a wall. The style of pointing chosen will considerably alter the look of a wall.

This unusual screen wall uses bricks in a design based on diagonals. The coping is complex, using specially moulded bricks and provides visual stability to the top of the run, while the vine softens the outline and frames the simple timber seat. Such a wall forms a practical screen, yet allows tantalizing glimpses of the surrounding garden.

Uses: As brick is a small module and easy to lay, its uses are almost limitless. Boundary walls are an obvious choice, but so, too, are screens and internal divisions, retaining walls, raised beds, water features, barbecues, steps, garden buildings, pillars to support pergolas, overheads and arbours, and many other features. Used as a boundary it will ensure continuity; used as an accent it provides punctuation. Brick walls can be straight or curved, staggered or interlocking. They form a superb backdrop to planting, and if facing the sun, will hold the heat to provide an added bonus for growing conditions. A pierced honeycomb wall will provide a delightful screen as well as making an effective windbreak, and because of the flexibility of the material, is as easy to construct as an arch. Brick can also be used as a frame for other, more random materials such as broken flint or stone.

Construction: All brick walls need sound foundations, or footings, twice as wide as the finished wall, and sufficiently deep to provide stability in the prevailing ground conditions. Footings should always be below the level of surrounding topsoil, and be taken down into undisturbed ground.

As a general rule, a wall that is built using a double layer of bricks both looks, and is, far stronger than a single thickness brick wall. The cost will be higher, but as a wall can stand for many hundreds of years, the initial outlay is well worthwhile. The pattern of bricks used in a wall is called the bond, and different bonds produce very different effects. These bonds give the wall its inherent strength, and the patterns are formed from stretchers (bricks laid along the face of the wall) and headers (bricks laid through the wall). It is unfortunately the case that bricklayers often use Flemish bond today, rather than English or English walling bond, both of which are visually rather more interesting.

Curved walls are inherently stronger than a straight run, and a staggered wall, with one right-angle butting into another, will be both strong and provide interesting bays and angles as a backdrop for planting. A long run will be subject to slight expansion and contraction in different temperatures, and it is prudent to incorporate expansion joints every 10–12m (32–40ft). In effect, this means that you will have a series of walls, separated by a gap about the width of your finger which will be filled either with a treated board or mastic.

Pointing, which keeps the weather out of the face of the bricks, has great visual impact, and should always be carried out neatly. Joints can be 'weathered' at an angle, 'rubbed back' to form a U-shaped joint, or 'raked out' to form a crisp shadow line that will emphasize the individual modules. When carrying out renovations, any new pointing should match the old.

While you probably will not need to worry about rising damp in garden walls, a suitable coping is necessary to keep the weather out of the top. By far the best coping for a brick wall is bricks laid on edge; this is simple, unpretentious, and does the job in hand. Occasionally you will see stone coping on brick walls. This can look superb but, unfortunately, it tends to cost a fortune. Well-made precast concrete coping is perfectly acceptable, but virtually anything else that may be suggested by your trendy architect should be avoided like the plague!

Contrasting & associating materials: Brick is the cosmopolitan of the landscape world, forming a superb background, or blending in with the widest possible range of other garden materials. There is a brick for every situation, whether it be a crisp, shiny engineering brick, or a rustic stock. The secret of success, as with everything else in the garden, is good design with a lack of ostentation and over-complication.

CONCRETE BLOCKS

The simple approach so often works best; these concrete blocks, laid to form a honeycomb wall, blend perfectly with the gate piers and the adjoining building. The gates themselves are great fun, the colour picking up that of the shutters.

Characteristics: Concrete blocks provide an eminently sensible and low-cost material for all types of walling. Blocks measure either 225 x 225 x 450mm (9 x 9 x 18in) or 100 x 225 x 450mm (4½ x 9 x 18in), the large size being the stronger, and have either a slightly rough or a smooth face. Blocks can either be rendered, painted or if constructed from an attractive aggregate, simply left as they are. Where new houses are built of the same material , concrete block boundary walls provide an ideal link between house and garden.

Uses: For freestanding and retaining walls and structures of all kinds. Their cheapness makes them especially suitable for a wide range of uses in utility areas of the garden. Laid with wide open joints they can be used to form a visually powerful 'honeycomb' wall. Their strength allows them to be used for high walls.

Construction: Sound foundations are essential, and should be twice as wide as the finished wall. Thinner blocks should only be used for fairly low walls, unless they are buttressed at regular intervals to give them additional strength. A simple stretcher bond is suitable for most walls. The best coping for a 225mm (9in) wall is brick laid on edge, while precast concrete coping is most suitable for a 100mm (4½in) wall. Pointing can either be flush, rubbed back or raked out. Alternatively, the surface can be painted or rendered.

Contrasting & associating materials: Concrete blocks usually look best in a contemporary setting, positioned alongside a house built in similar blocks or with rendered walls. Precast concrete paving, *in-situ* concrete, gravel and timber in the form of decking or railway sleepers are all compatible.

RENDERED CONCRETE

Characteristics: In Britain, but fortunately not in other parts of the world, concrete is considered a cheap and nasty material. Cheap it may be (which is in its favour); nasty it certainly is not.

Rendered concrete walls form one of the most durable and cost-effective boundaries or dividers available. Built with a low-cost core of brick or concrete blocks, they can be finished in a wide range of renders: textured, patterned, pebble-dashed with small stones just after the wet mix has been applied, or smooth – when it presents an ideal surface for painting. They are thus extremely adaptable, and can be blended into many different architectural and garden situations.

Uses: Rendered walls are the workhorse of many a garden, and are especially useful in a contemporary situation where adjoining buildings are also built of concrete. By using a colour wash, you can extend a colour scheme from inside to out, and produce an effect that is refreshingly clean and crisp. Such walls will also be an excellent low-cost choice for screening utility work areas or for use as retaining walls.

Construction: Sound foundations are needed, and should be twice as wide as the finished wall. The core should be built of brick or concrete blocks, and rendered to provide the final finish. A good coping is essential to keep the weather out of the top of the wall and prevent it loosening the render. Brick on edge is the best, but neat precast concrete is also suitable.

Contrasting & associating materials: Rendered walls often look best in conjunction with contemporary materials such as precast concrete paving, brushed aggregates, decking, and chunky timbers such as railway sleepers. They also associate well with crisp, well-detailed timber fences.

Don't be afraid to use strong tones. The warmth of this colour-washed and crudely rendered wall brightens up this courtyard and blends well with the terracotta tiles of the floor. Such a confident treatment will almost certainly reflect the character of the owner.

If you have the right setting, concrete can be one of the most visually organic materials at your disposal. This wall and gateway has an enormous feeling of strength and movement.

Rendering a surface not only softens the outline but can be used to create many other varied effects, some of which may reflect a strongly regional flavour.

IN SITU CONCRETE

Characteristics: Go to any American town or city, and you will see *in situ* concrete used in the most imaginative and elegant ways. It is immensely strong – truly the stone of the twentieth century. Because the walls require some kind of casing or shuttering to hold the wet concrete in place until it hardens, an infinite variety of finishes is possible. Heavily grained boards can be used to impart their pattern to the finished wall, and the boards themselves can be of varying widths and set at different depths to set up fascinating rhythms on the exposed surface. Alternatively, the surface can be mechanically hammered to create ribbed and indented patterns of all kinds. Runs need not be straight; curved concrete walls are easily built, which opens up all kinds of exciting design possibilities. The only important thing is to make sure that the wall is in keeping with its surroundings.

Uses: In situ concrete walls can be used in the widest possible range of situations. Although normally used in contemporary designs, they can, if great design skill is exercised, be used to superb effect alongside traditional materials or in historic settings. Walls like these can form an obvious extension to a house built of similar materials, and would be an excellent choice for retaining walls and other load-bearing structures.

Construction: These walls are cast in their entirety, including the foundations below ground level, and steel reinforcing rods are often used to give internal strength. Walls can be either vertical or battered (tapered), and shuttering will be required to hold the wet concrete in place. This is usually timber – either boards or large sheets of plywood – and must in turn be held in place by a framework of timbers. Thorough compaction of the concrete, often with a mechanical vibrator, is essential at all stages as it is poured, and the shuttering must not be struck (removed) until the wall has hardened completely.

Contrasting & associating materials: Since it is so versatile, *in situ* concrete can associate with virtually anything around it. The critical factor is the sympathetic design of the wall.

This is a restrained, low maintenance composition with a Japanese influence. The utter simplicity of the smooth concrete walling, impeccably fitted around the old tree, provides the perfect link with the adjoining house.

There are certain situations in which gardens, or parts of gardens, can be left completely free of plants. This is a stunningly simple and powerful use of concrete, as well as being a study in colour, form, texture and shape.

ALTERNATIVE MATERIALS

This is pure abstract art, using a variety of different materials, patterns and colours to build up an overall picture that runs on either side of a heating duct. So often such a situation would be handled in a far less imaginative way.

Characteristics: Walls can be built from all kinds of materials in addition to the ones mentioned above. You only need to look around you to see the possibilities. The great architect Sir Edwin Lutyens, a master of the vernacular, employed a wide range of local materials to superb effect; these included slate and tiles used with intricate detailing to frame panels of brick or stone. Honeycomb walls, usually constructed from bricks with a gap left between each, can also be made from clay land drains, with one course stacked on top of the next and carefully mortared in position. Half-round ridge tiles can be used to create screen walls, or dividers, and create a far more handsome effect than the dire pressed concrete examples that I propose to ignore in this book. You can see superb examples of tile walls throughout the Mediterranean.

On a more contemporary note, glass blocks can be a lot of fun; they distort the image, allow light to filter through, and look fine in the right setting. I have myself used concrete lintels set vertically in the ground to form a fascinating screen, varying the height of the tops to set up terrific rhythms. The real point is to use your imagination. I am waiting for a client bold enough to allow me to build a glass or acrylic wall filled with oil that is heated and lit from below. The effect at night would be simply stunning, with bubbles rising and falling in great amoebic shapes!

Uses: Alternative walls can be used almost anywhere. The prime rule is sensitive design and lateral thinking – as well as a sense of humour!

Construction: This will vary according to the materials chosen.

Contrasting & associating materials: Variable; contemporary or traditional. It is worth remembering that hi-tech materials can look brilliant in an historic setting. It is a shame that few people have the ability or the courage to experiment in this direction.

Glass blocks have been used here to form a light and attractive screen, the distortion being enough to prevent a direct view through the boundary. The main psychological problem that may need to be overcome here is the feeling that you are being looked at!

PANEL FENCES

Interwoven panels, and variations on the theme, can form an excellent and neutral boundary once they have weathered down. Ivy is a fine climber, particularly in shade, but needs to be prevented from forcing its way between slats and causing damage.

Characteristics: Panel fences are relatively cheap, easy to erect, and last for anything from ten to twenty years, provided they are properly maintained. Most are made from interwoven slats of thin timber, set within a frame and fixed between posts set firmly in the ground. The length of each panel is usually 1.8m (6ft), but the height can be anything from 900mm (3ft) to 1.8m (6ft).

Most panels are pre-treated with preservative, but the colour is often very pale, making them glaringly obvious. The secret is to tone them down with a darker preservative, allowing them to merge into the landscape and providing a better backdrop for planting. Panel fences should be unobtrusive, and not, like some other fences, used as a feature in their own right; their visual strength lies in their uniformity, providing a neutral background that does not shout for attention.

Uses: As boundaries, dividers, screens for utility areas, fencing for dog runs, and many other kinds of enclosure. Being solid, they can provide privacy, and they are strong enough to keep people or animals in or out.

Construction: Panels are fixed to posts that are either concreted into the ground or slotted into metal shoes. The tops of the posts should be capped and kept flush with the panels. Each panel, topped with a capping rail, should be fitted at about 150mm (6in) above ground level to minimize rotting – the gap may be bridged by replaceable gravel boards nailed between the posts. Apply an annual coat of non-toxic preservative (never creosote, which will damage plants) to both panels and posts.

Contrasting & associating materials: If stained the right colour, they will blend into a wide range of situations.

ERECTING A PANEL FENCE
Panels are widely available and they are easy to erect between posts to make one of the cheapest of fences.

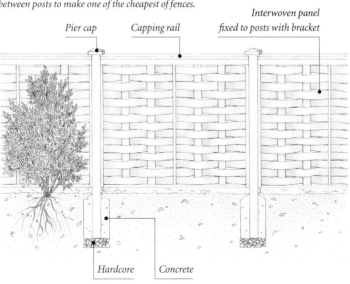

Pier cap
Capping rail
Interwoven panel fixed to posts with bracket
Hardcore
Concrete

CONCRETE SPUR
Attach concrete spurs to the bases of timber posts to prevent them from rotting. Gravel boards running between posts can easily be replaced if they start to decay.

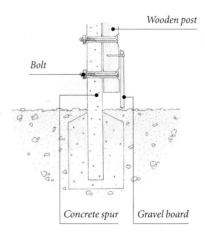

Wooden post
Bolt
Concrete spur
Gravel board

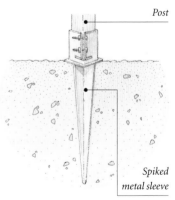

Post
Spiked metal sleeve

METAL POST SUPPORT
Metal spikes must be driven absolutely vertically into the ground. This task can be made simpler by using adjustable supports.

CLOSE BOARD FENCES

This is an attractive and unusual variation on a close board fence, where wide and narrow boards are set alternately, the latter bridging the gap and providing additional vertical emphasis. Such fences can be painted to blend with the house or another colour scheme.

CONSTRUCTING A CLOSE BOARD FENCE

Close board fences are more expensive than panels, but normally last longer and can conform to sloping or rolling ground.

Capping rail (optional)   Overlapping feather-edged boards   Arris rails

Gravel board   Hardcore   Concrete

Characteristics: Close board fences belong to the large family of fences in which individual slats or boards are nailed vertically to horizontal rails set between posts. They are strong, durable, unobtrusive, provide privacy, and form excellent secure boundaries. Height is usually 1.8m (6ft), but may be more. They are more complicated to erect than panel fences, the work usually being carried out by specialist contractors, and the cost is therefore correspondingly greater. As with any outdoor timber constructions, they should be treated regularly with a non-toxic preservative to prevent rot.

Uses: Primarily as medium-cost secure boundaries. Close board is particularly suited to sloping or undulating ground, where the fence can follow the contours of the land. Because boards are fitted individually, they can allow for a tree or other feature to protrude through the boundary fence – something that is impossible with a panel fence.

Construction: Posts must be fixed securely into the ground 1.8m (6ft) apart, set in concrete, with two or three horizontal arris rails slotted into mortices cut in the posts. The overlapping boards are usually 150mm (6in) wide and feather-edged, which means that the thickness tapers from one side to the other. The top of the run is not normally capped, but replaceable gravel boards are fitted at the bottom.

Contrasting & associating materials: Like panel fences, close board fences are intended to provide an unobtrusive background, and should be stained to achieve this. They are particularly successful in a woodland setting, where the vertical line blends well with trees.

This close board fence has been fitted above a low wall of burnt bricks topped with a crisp engineering-brick coping. Such a treatment could easily have ended up as a muddle, but it works well, the strong colour drawing the gate and house into the composition.

SLATTED FENCES

This highly individualistic slatted fence has been specifically designed to fit a particular situation. The rhythm of the swooping cut-outs is echoed on a smaller scale by the balls on the tops of the posts.

slats create a feeling of space – a particularly useful design tool in a small garden. As well as varying the width of boards, you can also vary the height of the fence; this can be especially pertinent for screens and dividers. Design permutations are many and various, boards can be set diagonally as well as horizontally or vertically, and here you can stamp your own individuality on to your boundary or internal divider – provided you carry out your plans with sensitivity and respect for your neighbours.

Uses: Slatted fences are almost invariably used as a contemporary design element, and generally look their best in such situations. For inspiration, look around you at well-conceived housing developments, or at places where good garden designers or landscape architects have been at work.

Construction: Much the same as for close board fences. The slats are nailed to arris rails fixed between posts, and here precision is of paramount importance: any misalignment of slats will look dreadful. It is also worth remembering that the thinner each individual slat, the more prone the timber will be to twisting and moving – a strong argument in favour of using well-seasoned hardwood from a reliable and renewable source.

Contrasting & associating materials: Slatted fences associate well with most modern materials. But designer fences look best in well-designed gardens – take heed!

CONSTRUCTING A SLATTED FENCE

It is possible to build slatted fences to the widest range of patterns, using boards of different widths. The direction of boards will provide visual emphasis.

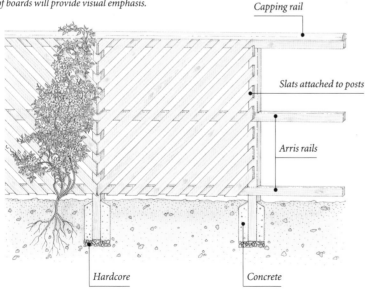

Capping rail

Slats attached to posts

Arris rails

Hardcore

Concrete

Characteristics: Vertically slatted fences use posts and arris rails, but instead of one board overlapping the next, there is usually a gap between each. Horizontally fitted boards are simply fitted to the posts without any intermediate support. Timber is normally sawn and planed, providing a crisp architectural finish which can be either painted, to pick up a colour scheme on the house, or stained.

Slats may be broad, narrow, or a subtle mixture of both. Wider boards will provide a greater degree of privacy, but it is worth remembering that wide boards are visually dominant and tend to draw a boundary in, while narrow, delicate

PICKET FENCES

This is a classic example of the picket fence that has come to epitomize the typical cottage garden with its simple line and undemonstrative nature. These pickets have been painted in traditional crisp white, and the posts have been screwed securely to the rails to prevent them from twisting out of their strict formation.

This is an unusual variation on a picket fence, with a Japanese theme. Such fences are common in the Far East, but have a strong vernacular character that can be difficult to handle out of context. The method of fixing posts to rails is an integral part of the design.

Characteristics: Picket fences provide well-loved boundaries for period or cottage front gardens or yards. Usually relatively low – about 1m (3ft) in height – and often painted white, they offer no privacy and little in the way of shelter; most dogs can jump straight over them. Tops can be cut square, pointed, or rounded, and are sometimes pierced with fancy slots – a fussy and unnecessary detail.

Uses: Really only as demarcation. They can be used to pick up the colour and style of the house, especially if this is of timber construction, and can look a good deal more lively if painted in one of the stronger primary colours rather than the ubiquitous white.

Construction: These are simple to build. Posts are set approximately 1.2m (4ft) apart, with pickets fixed to two horizontal rails. Pickets should be the same height as the posts, and should be kept just clear of the ground. Gaps should be slightly narrower than the pickets.

Contrasting & associating materials: The ideal setting for these fences has almost become a cliché: old brick paths, natural stone paving, gravel, and masses of herbaceous planting. I need say no more!

RANCH FENCES

SINGLE RAIL FENCES

Ranch fences need not necessarily be the crisp white-painted affairs so common in suburban areas. A variation on the theme can often be seen in a more rural setting, as here, where the boards are left unpainted and simply nailed to the posts in a far less formal way.

An unusual but interesting example of a single rail fence; such a design would need to be positioned in a garden where a similar style of timberwork provided an overall theme. This example is both the right height and strong enough to double as an occasional seat.

Characteristics: Ranch fences use wide horizontal boards instead of vertical ones, but still with a slight gap between each. They are reminiscent of the architecture of the sixties and seventies, and provided this looks good, so do they. They also look fine adjoining contemporary buildings, and provide a strong visual plane that can extend the clean lines of the house out into the garden.

Boards can be nailed to one side of the posts, or set alternately behind and in front – a technique known as 'hit and miss'. Fences are normally 1.8m (6ft) high, or more; in front gardens and yards they may be lower. They are often painted white, and this needs regular attention if the fences are not to look slightly seedy.

Uses: Ranch fences generally look better when used as boundaries rather than as dividers, but can be useful as a utility screen to run at right angles off a boundary.

Construction: Posts are set 1.8m (6ft) apart, and boards are planed smooth and should run absolutely horizontally. If the ground slopes, the fence should be stepped in sections.

Contrasting & associating materials: These fences look best in contemporary situations and alongside contemporary materials. They associate particularly well with overhead beams, especially if they have been constructed from similar planks and painted the same colour.

Characteristics: Sometimes known as trip rails, these fences are usually no more than 600mm (2ft) high, and are often lower. Rails can be constructed from square section timber set into a V-groove in the top of the posts, or from metal tubes threaded through the posts.

Uses: Usually used as demarcation for front gardens, to prevent parking; or at the back of the house in situations where there is no need for a solid boundary (which might interrupt a fine view), and where privacy is not important. They can be used in contemporary and traditional situations. You will often see excellent examples in public open spaces such as parks.

Construction: Posts are set 1.8m (6ft) apart. Where rails are set in a groove, a metal strip the same width as the post is tacked to one side of the post, taken over both the rail and the groove, and nailed to the post on either side. Where a metal rail runs through the post, the top of the post can simply be neatly rounded off. If the construction is entirely of timber then this is normally stained; where a metal rail is used, the latter can be painted, perhaps to pick up a colour scheme elsewhere.

Contrasting & associating materials: A simple fence like this is very undemanding, and will blend with a wide range of contemporary and traditional settings and materials.

POST & RAIL FENCES

I can't help thinking of Huckleberry Finn when I see this type of post and rail fence! This beautifully weathered example suits its situation perfectly, blending well both with the area and surrounding buildings. The poppies are something else!

Characteristics: The over-used fence of paddocks, with horses gazing over the top, and of pretentious gardens that can boast of anything approaching a good view. Although relatively cheap and easy to erect, if used in inappropriate surroundings post and rail fences can be dreadfully obtrusive. They should, if possible, be hidden in a fold in the ground, or, if the budget will allow, replaced by a ha-ha or iron park fence. If you must have them, leave them natural; painted white, they are even worse.

Uses: They are really only suitable for keeping large animals such as horses and cattle out of the garden. Even these will either jump them or force their way through if they are sufficiently determined. You will have to nail sheep wire between the posts if you wish to keep smaller animals out or children in.

Construction: Fences can be either two- or three-rail, and are usually about 1.2m (4ft) high. Rough-sawn posts should be set approximately 1.8m (6ft) apart, and the cleft rails set in mortices. Hardwoods are the most durable choice.

Contrasting & associating materials: The strongly rural flavour of these fences means that they should be used only in the country, alongside lawns, grassland or crops. If you plant next to them, animals will lean over and eat the lot.

POST & ROPE FENCES

This is an excellent example of how posts and ropes should be put together, using solid uprights and double swags of cable. There is little privacy afforded by such a boundary, but it provides a wonderful vehicle for climbing plants of all kinds.

Characteristics: Very occasionally you will see post and rope fencing used like single rail fencing: low and as a demarcation. More often, it is used above eye level as a superb divider, and as a support for climbing roses and other climbers. Either one or two ropes can be used as swags; if a single rope is used, it must be a stout one or the feature will look flimsy.

Uses: This traditional garden feature, much loved by Gertrude Jekyll and her contemporaries, can have a thoroughly modern treatment. I have occasionally used brightly coloured rope slung between equally bright poles! Although more often used as a divider, posts and ropes can also be run along the back of a border, used to flank a path, or to provide vertical emphasis around a focal point such as a circular pool or sunken garden.

Construction: Every aspect needs to be sturdy: posts should be at least 150mm (6in) square, and 1.8m (6ft) high and ropes at least 25mm (1in) thick. Ropes are threaded through holes in the posts, and it is essential to ensure that posts are the same distance apart, and that each loop is the same length.

Contrasting & associating materials: Usually best in a traditional setting, surrounded by complementary natural materials; occasionally effective in a hi-tech design, with synthetic and man-made items.

BAMBOO FENCES

This is the real thing, a proper Japanese garden with a superb bamboo screen, which encourages 'borrowed' landscape from the area beyond, and provides a strong physical boundary at the same time. The lashings are an integral part of the design.

Characteristics: These fences are traditionally found in the Far East where they are used in much the same way as reed in this country. You only need to visit Japan or study pictures of gardens in that part of the world to see what an elegant boundary the material makes.

Fences can be high, and closely woven from thin stems to provide privacy and shelter, or made as a much more open structure, using thicker stems to form a screen or open boundary.

Uses: Either as boundaries, or as screens or dividers within the garden. They do, however, have quite strong oriental connotations, so need careful handling if they are not to look rather ostentatious.

Construction: Closely woven fencing of this kind is usually available in panels, and can be carefully wired to stout bamboo posts driven into the ground. Screens are normally made up on site from lengths of bamboo cut to size and tied to posts. They are best, and traditionally, tied on to the posts with twine – which needs to conform to a set pattern to be technically correct.

Contrasting & associating materials: Solid bamboo fences have a simplicity of line that makes them look comfortable in many contemporary settings. They also make a superb backdrop for all kinds of planting. Bamboo screens will really only look correct in a garden that has strong Japanese overtones.

On this delightful roof garden, thin bamboo canes have been laced together to form panels and set behind a stout timber framework. Such fencing provides attractive, unobtrusive shelter and makes the perfect background for planting of all kinds.

WATTLE, OSIER & REED FENCES

Reed fences provide a simple, unobtrusive and practical background and are used here to form an architectural enclosure for a pretty little parterre. As the weave is delicate, the seat is thrown into sharp contrast, providing the major focal point in the composition.

Whether they are made from split or whole stems, woven wattle hurdles provide an unobtrusive background that makes an ideal foil to plants. Panels normally measure 1.8 x 1.8m (6 x 6ft) and will last for approximately ten years.

Characteristics: Wattle hurdles and osier or reed fences are all hand-made from local materials. Wattle hurdles, made from woven hazel stems, were originally used to pen sheep, and measure about 1.8m (6ft) square. They can be used to make a superb rural boundary that will provide an unobtrusive backdrop for planting. Their life-expectancy is only about ten years, but this is normally sufficient for a border or a hedge to have reached maturity. Only a few skilled craftsmen produce them today, so they are relatively expensive.

Osier panels are much the same as wattles, but use willow stems which are thinner and therefore have a finer visual texture. Reed fences are traditionally made in fen or river lowland areas where reeds grow naturally, and are sometimes made *in situ*. The reeds are usually sandwiched between timber rails.

Uses: Although these fences look most at home in the country, they can also be effective in a strongly urban situation and against contemporary architecture. They all provide a complete screen, making them ideal for boundaries.

Construction: Panels are simply wired to round posts driven well into the ground.

Contrasting & associating materials: Because of their natural appearance and subtle texture, all these fences look handsome in a wide range of situations and against an equally wide range of materials, both traditional and contemporary.

The texture of woven osiers is delicate and delightful, so too is the colour, but their life is limited and they are only suitable for relatively short-term use. The shadows set up endless patterns, forming a perfect backdrop to a border.

PARK FENCES

Park fences are the ultimate retainers of a fine view, and when painted black, hardly distract from the landscape beyond. They have a long life and this example has been fitted with thinner wire for extra security.

Characteristics: Metal park fences are the forerunners of timber post and rail fences, are used in similar situations, and, if you can afford them, are a far better proposition. You can still see long runs in parkland or along the edges of estates. The steel elements (originally iron) are considerably thinner than timber, and consequently far less visually intrusive; painted black, they become almost invisible. Most fences are 1.2m (4ft) high and are relatively stock proof, but higher ones are sometimes required to keep deer in or out and these may be curved inwards at the top.

Uses: This type of fencing is still being produced, and is the perfect answer to a fine view. Even set against the horizon it will barely disrupt it. It can often be used more cheaply for short runs, perhaps where a garden drifts out into woodland between two wings of planting.

Construction: Uprights consisting of a steel strip splayed out at the bottom should be set in concrete below ground level to provide stability. Three or four horizontal rails, either round or formed of a lighter strip, are then threaded through the uprights; a greater number will be needed for higher deer fences.

Contrasting & associating materials: Such a fence will usually be set in grassland, or between informal wings of planting, where it will look perfect – and as unobtrusive as possible.

WROUGHT & CAST IRON FENCES

Wrought iron is infinitely variable, looking equally at home in town or country. This screen and hooped pergola allows planting to scramble gently over the structure and encroach on the adjoining garden in a deliciously informal manner.

Characteristics: Traditional wrought iron fences are usually superb, principally because of the craftsmanship involved and the quality of the materials used. If you have such a fence or divider, cherish it and maintain it well; it is priceless. The highly skilled craft of metal-working, where strips are fashioned and joined together, is making something of a comeback, and it is possible to obtain fine new fencing today, but it is extremely expensive. The advantage of a contemporary metal screen will be its delicacy and visual lightness. If you find the right thing, and can afford it, go for it! Popular low-cost contemporary versions are unfortunately a travesty of the real thing, and nearly always look over-complicated and flimsy.

Cast iron was much loved by the Victorians, and many fine fences still remain, though many British examples were melted down for weapons during World War II. Unfortunately, it is brittle, and once broken is almost impossible to repair.

Uses: All are suitable for fences, railings and dividers, though in different situations. Metal railings can look superb in conjunction with, or on top of a wall.

Construction: This is in the hands of craftsmen, and unless you own a foundry or a forge is beyond the average person's capability. Fixing such fences must also be left to the specialist landscape designer.

Contrasting & associating materials: Metal fences like these usually associate best with traditional settings and natural materials. Modern designs can obviously work well in a contemporary situation.

CORRUGATED IRON FENCES

Historically, corrugated iron has a bad name, which is a pity as the modern forms can be used as worthwhile boundaries. It can be cut on an angle to match a slope, and here it provides a powerful link with the colour of the boards on the house.

Characteristics: Corrugated iron has long been used as utility fencing, but variations on the theme have brought it thoroughly up to date.

Uses: Sheet metal can be bent to various patterns and shapes, which can set up fascinating surface shadows. Colour can be imparted during the manufacturing process or painted after erection to link with a colour scheme on the house or elsewhere in the garden.

Construction: Metal posts should be concreted into the ground, with the corrugated iron panels bolted between them.

Contrasting & associating materials: Best in a contemporary setting with crisp, man-made materials.

Cast iron, or more often today, cast alloy, forms an elegant boundary, albeit one that provides little privacy. With this type of fence, planting can be encouraged to soften the line, blending the boundary out into the wider garden or landscape.

POST & CHAIN

Post and chain fences provide a sophisticated and traditional fence outside many a period property, although they offer little in the way of privacy. The posts can be painted, as here, to provide an effective visual link with adjacent paintwork.

Characteristics: Another fine traditional fence, which uses low timber posts or stone bollards with interlinking wrought iron chains. These are usually found at the front of fine period houses or flanking driveways, and are used as demarcation. Look around you for inspiration. Garden centres that sell plastic versions should be liquidated!

Uses: This elegant divider has no security or practical value, though it can be useful for preventing inconsiderate parking.

Construction: Posts are usually only about 450mm (18in) high, concreted into the ground, and are fitted with iron hooks just below the top. Chains are traditionally made from spiked links, though you will see other versions. Stone posts or bollards are usually craftsman-made, but are now also being manufactured in reconstituted stone.

Contrasting & associating materials: At their best in traditional settings, near similar materials. Can look superb set in grass or stone paving.

CHAIN LINK

Occasionally, one fence type can be used in conjunction with another: here chain link has been set behind old iron railings to provide an impassable screen. It is remarkable just how unobtrusive chain link can be when used in an appropriate setting.

Characteristics: An underrated fence, all too often considered only in terms of security. It is certainly almost unsurpassed for this purpose, but can also be used as a boundary that allows a view to run into the garden. The only satisfactory version is one with plastic-coated posts and wire, and if these are brown or black, rather than the ubiquitous green, the fence will become almost invisible in the landscape. Height can vary from relatively low (the useless dividers that are found so often on housing estates) to high, for high security.

Uses: As an unobtrusive boundary, best sited at some distance from the house. Perfect, too, around a tennis court (here, again, brown or black is better than green). It is particularly effective behind tall planting, or running into woodland, where the mesh becomes almost invisible. It can provide support for twining plants, which can hide the fence completely. It can also be used behind an open fence, providing security for pets and children, as well as plant support.

Construction: Chain link fencing will be supplied with everything you need. Posts will need concreting into the ground, and straining posts are often set at the ends of runs, or where the run turns through a right angle, and are bolted into the uprights to provide added strength. The chain link is connected to the uprights with metal strips threaded through the mesh and then bolted to the posts.

Contrasting & associating materials: The secret with chain link is that it should be invisible. If it is blatantly obvious it really becomes pretty difficult to associate it with anything apart from a scrapyard.

SYNTHETICS & REPRODUCTION TIMBER

Characteristics: One of the reasons why most garden design is about fifty years behind every other art form is because of our stubborn resistance to using synthetics in the garden. Ignoring the existence of plastics, polyesters and man-made fibres, is frankly a form of horticultural snobbery, and the problem is compounded by the fact that garden centres do not sell them, and most garden designers haven't a clue about using them. Not only is there nothing wrong with using these materials, there are enormous assets. They come in all kinds of exciting colours and textures, as well as being virtually indestructible, and I have had a lot of fun, and some success, experimenting with them myself.

One of the best synthetic fencing materials is the woven polyester used for cricket sight screens. It is light, rot-proof and translucent (which means that there is no problem with a shaded border). It is clipped into lightweight alloy panels bolted to alloy uprights. Unfortunately, it is only available in white; primary colours would be more exciting.

Nurserymen have long used windbreaks of tough plastic webbing stretched between timber posts, and this, too, could have a use in the domestic garden as a neutral (and completely rot-proof) background. I have also used thin plastic poles, set close together, as dividers. These *are* available in bright colours, and you can vary the height of the tops, swooping them up or down. They also sway in the wind, setting up their own rhythm and sounds. In other words, think laterally: it's fun, and you could be on to something new.

Recycling is in vogue – quite rightly so – and there is now reproduction timber on the market that ingeniously solves the problem of what to do with spent polystyrene. It looks almost identical to wood, is just as strong and, although being relatively expensive, will last considerably longer than many natural timbers, being virtually rot-proof. It is normally available in boards of varying width and thickness, and also comes in a wide range of colours, which makes it useful to designers working with an overall theme in mind.

Uses: Alternative materials such as these can be used for both fences and screens. Reproduction timber can replace natural timbers in virtually all their applications, including overheads, pergolas, fencing and specialist woodworking. Because of its relatively high cost, it is best suited to high profile projects, and would not be an economic option for more mundane carpentry.

Construction: You may need to work this out as you go. As with any job in the garden, fixings need to be secure and long-lasting. Reproduction timber is slightly harder than most natural timbers, but the carpentry skills required are identical.

Contrasting & associating materials: Most of the suggestions above will look best in a contemporary design, alongside contemporary materials. Just as with conventional timber, reproduction timber can be used for the widest possible range of purposes and design situations.

Reproduction timber looks pretty much the same as the real thing, but it is far more durable and comes in a wide range of colours. These overheads and trellis are an excellent example of its versatility and stability.

METAL GATES

Wrought iron work at its best is simply superb, having a delicacy and lightness of line that is impossible to achieve with other materials. Here the entire composition is in harmony, railings and gate being designed as one.

Characteristics: Metal is an expensive material, and suspiciously cheap metal gates, like cheap metal railings, are rarely worth the money – especially if set in a mediocre wall of reconstituted stone. There is nothing to beat a fine old wrought iron gate, and these can be found in all sizes from a simple pedestrian gate to a huge and elaborate one set in a wall at the entrance to a country estate. The important thing is that it should be right for its purpose; it is easy to be ostentatious!

Virtually all metal gates allow you to see straight through them, which may allow you to appreciate a fine view (in either direction) but will not provide any privacy.

Uses: Metal gates can be used for pedestrian or vehicle access in situations where privacy is not important and where they are intended to last. They have obvious uses in traditional settings, but some stunning designs are now being produced, in both wrought iron and steel, that will enhance contemporary settings. They are ideal for linking dividers within the garden framework, heightening tension as you move between the different areas, and preventing access where necessary (for children or pets) while maintaining a view.

Construction: Metal gates require highly skilled work by a blacksmith, or foundry, to individually designed or existing patterns.

Contrasting & associating materials: Metal gates usually look best set in substantial brick or stone boundaries; these have the visual strength to carry the fine detailing successfully. The setting can be traditional or contemporary, with materials to match.

HANGING A METAL GATE
Always check the clearance of the gate before concreting the post in position. If there is sloping ground this must be allowed for, otherwise the gate will scratch the surface every time it is opened.

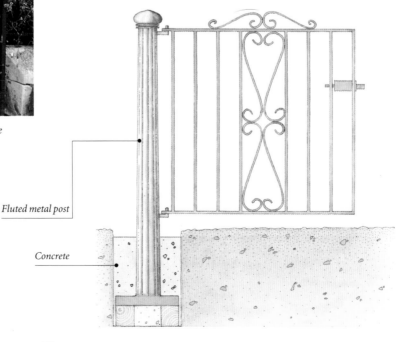

Fluted metal post

Concrete

There are places and situations you can simply dream about; in this setting all the various elements work beautifully together to form a stunning overall picture.

The juxtaposition of the boldly coloured vases and the delicately worked iron gates is pure magic; such is the stuff of outstanding design.

KISSING GATES

MOON GATES

Metal kissing gates have a great feeling of delicacy and lightness, which is heightened when they are set within a boundary constructed from brick or stone, as here. Well constructed examples will last almost indefinitely.

This is an unusual moon gate in that it provides access through the boundary. There is a telling contrast between the solidity of the old brick wall and the much more delicate gate and railings. The view is an attractive one, drawing you into the next garden room.

Characteristics: A charming and romantic way for pedestrians to pass through a boundary. The gate pivots within a framework, allowing one person to pass through at a time. If two attempt it, they get stuck – hence the name!

Normally waist-height, kissing gates are made either of timber or metal, and are usually designed to match the adjoining boundary. Both timber and metal kissing gates are found in low stone and brick walls.

Uses: As occasional gates into woodland or an adjoining field, or from one part of the garden to another. They are a prime example of a feature that affects the speed of movement through a space, and can be a useful design tool.

Construction: Timber is obviously easier to handle than metal, but both will need skilled workmanship. In both cases the design should be as unobtrusive and simple as possible.

Contrasting & associating materials: Metal kissing gates are purpose-made to match park fencing and, like the fencing, will look good with traditional and natural materials. Wooden gates blend most readily with fencing of the same material. Contemporary gates, made to crisp patterns and painted, look fine with similarly modern materials.

Characteristics: These are not gates as such, but holes – usually circular – pierced in garden boundaries or dividers to embrace a view. This is an old landscape device, originating in the Far East, and moon gates need positioning with great skill; they are not features to be overdone!

Moon gates can be set in brick, stone, or even well-designed fencing. The hole is usually left open, but attractive wooden shutters can be incorporated for security, privacy or shelter. Metal grilles can also be used, though these will not provide privacy or a windbreak.

Uses: As a landscape device; they have great aesthetic value in the right setting, and a good view is of course essential. Moon gates are sometimes used, with mirrors positioned behind them, as a visual trick in small town gardens; this may be a clever idea, but it tends to smack of affectation.

Construction: Moon gates need to be substantial to be effective, and usually have a diameter of 1.8m (6ft) or more. The circumference of the circle should be finished in the same coping as that used for the boundary. If introduced into a timber fence the opening will need to be carefully cut out. Like the boundary itself, moon gates will probably require the skills of a specialist bricklayer or stonemason. Wooden shutters can be quite straightforward to make; metal ones will require an expert.

Contrasting & associating materials: This will depend on the setting. Moon gates can be designed to suit both traditional and more contemporary gardens.

WOODEN GATES

A sense of fun is an invaluable part of good garden design, and this charming rustic gate is full of character. The colour combination is subtle and there is an initiative test incorporated in the design – how to undo the rope at the base!

Characteristics: The majority of boundaries are made from timber, and gates follow suit. As in all areas of design, simple solutions almost always work best: a straightforward ledge and brace design looks fine in a close board fence; a solid door looks best in a brick wall; and a picket-style gate suits a fence of a similar kind. Both hard and soft woods are used; both must be treated regularly with non-toxic preservative, or painted.

Pedestrian gates are sometimes combined with those for vehicles, the smaller side gate opens for people, the other for vehicles. Timber gates of this kind are often of the five-bar variety, and, again, the design should be kept simple; there are some elaborate shockers out there, and they are expensive to boot!

Uses: Simple timber gates, being so adaptable as well as cost-effective, can be used in virtually any situation, whether traditional or contemporary.

Construction: The simplest designs can be tackled by most people with basic carpentry skills and the right tools. More complex designs may require more sophisticated skills.

Contrasting & associating materials: There is really no limit to where or the materials alongside which such gates can be used; it is simply open to good design sense and imagination.

Some gardens and boundaries are simple and easy going, and this delightful picket gate reinforces the relaxed surroundings. The old brick path meanders towards the entrance and the latter allows the view to drift through and above the boundary.

TRELLIS

Often, the simplest things work best of all in a garden: this straightforward squared trellis acts both as a divider between different areas of the composition and as a practical and attractive support for climbing plants.

CONSTRUCTING A TRELLIS DIVIDER

Trellis is available in panels of varying height that can be fixed between posts.

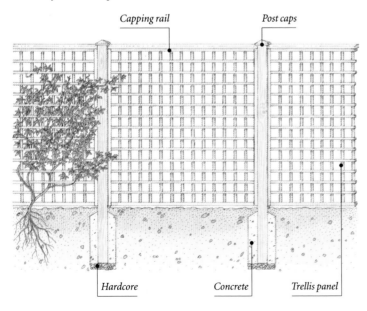

Capping rail   Post caps

Hardcore   Concrete   Trellis panel

Characteristics: Trellis is essentially an open structure, usually of timber though occasionally of metal, that allows the view to run through it while providing an ideal host for climbing plants. It comes in a variety of patterns, most of which are based on a diamond, rectangle, or square; you can even find one pattern of slats laid upon another, but a simple squared matrix probably forms the best background for plants. Lighter or heavier effects are achieved by the use of thinner or thicker slats in proportion to the gaps in between, and sturdier hardwood trellis (traditionally chestnut) is used for garden buildings. Standard panels are available from garden centres, and are usually 1.8m (6ft) square, but you can also get variations to fit specific situations, and tops may be scalloped or swept up into arched shapes of various kinds. Trellis is either painted or stained with preservative. Metal trellis is unusual, but you will find thick plastic-coated wire that although strong, looks flimsy.

Uses: Trellis is one of the best dividers at the garden designer's disposal, and its delicacy makes it ideal for extending the line of a boundary unobtrusively into the garden. Wings of trellis, fronted by planting, are part of the essence of a traditional English country garden, and have the advantage of casting little shade.

Trellis can be used to raise the height of a boundary, and is often used on top of relatively low walls to improve privacy. It can also be used as panels on walls to support climbing plants, although horizontal wires are usually a better and more practical choice, and instead of low hedging to frame beds. In the more mundane parts of the garden, trellis can be used to screen utility areas or garden buildings. The fruit garden is an area in which trellis can be both practical and decorative, acting as a host for espaliers, cordons, vines and cane fruits. Such an area need not be simply a utility space, trellis can make it far more decorative, and draw it into the wider garden composition.

Construction: All too often, trellis panels look and are far too flimsy, and are made from untreated timber that is prone to rot. An ideal timber size for most trellis work is just under 20mm (¾in) square, while hardwood trellis looks better and will last for an exceptionally long time. Panels are fixed to posts, which are often supplied by the manufacturer in a specific pattern to match the trellis, and will need concreting into the ground or fitting with spiked metal shoes. The finished article can be either pre-painted by the supplier (an increasingly popular option) or stained with preservative.

Contrasting & associating materials: Trellis is an accommodating medium and fits comfortably into a wide range of situations, both urban and rural. The more contrived patterns need to be handled carefully, and blended into an appropriate garden style. Ready-stained trellis has become popular recently and can be obtained in a wide range of different shades. While this can justifiably link with adjoining colour schemes it is often used simply to be fashionable, which is *not* the best reason.

FEDGES

Fedges can play host to a wide range of plants, whether pelargoniums, as here, or species that lean against a surface, such as chaenomeles, climbers, or annuals. The latter can either be contained in pots, hung on the frame or, if sufficiently rampant, trained from ground level.

CONSTRUCTING A FEDGE
This is a flexible feature and can be built to virtually any pattern. Sink hardwood posts approximately 450mm (18in) into the ground, before tacking on lengths of chicken wire or chain link fencing.

Characteristics: A fedge is a hybrid between a fence and a hedge. It is made from some kind of framework, over which a scrambling climber such as honeysuckle or ivy is grown. It looks like a hedge, but is far quicker to establish.

Uses: This device is ideal as a divider within a garden, and is usually best kept under 1.5m (5ft) in height. Above this, climbers tend to become leggy and die out at the bottom.

Construction: The simplest frame consists of two rows of posts, approximately 600mm (2ft) apart in either direction, joined at the top by wires, and with wires running horizontally between them. Chicken wire or chain link fencing is then stretched over the whole thing and tacked down firmly. Finally, climbers are planted on either side, tied in as they grow, and quickly colonize the structure. Maintenance is confined to careful clipping or pruning.

Fedges are close relations of topiary, and ambitious practitioners can experiment with the final structural outline by modifying the underlying framework.

Contrasting & associating materials: Fedges will easily link with the overall style of the garden, whether this be traditional or contemporary, urban or rural, and, depending on the plant material used, can readily associate with hard or soft landscape materials.

FORMAL HEDGES

High drama is an integral part of many a fine garden, and this simple composition has immense power, generated by the high walls of beech that lead the eye down to the plain seat at the end of the vista. This is visual tension at its strongest.

Characteristics: Species that can be clipped to provide a crisp, unified appearance such as yew and box are obvious and traditional contenders for formal internal dividers and boundaries. The berries of yew are poisonous and this should be taken into consideration if there will be children in the garden or livestock in adjoining fields. Box or yew will make a stunning foil for pale planting, white seats, and spring blossom. In a large garden, more textured beech, hornbeam, holly, privet, lonicera, even Leyland cypress can also be used as dividers, and form excellent boundary material.

Uses: Hedges are far more adaptable than fences or walls, and can be laid out, clipped, or allowed to grow, in any number of different shapes and patterns. The top of a boundary or screen can be scalloped or crenellated, and wings can swoop down to meet a path, heightening tension as you approach. Topiary ornaments can be introduced along their tops, and arches are easily formed. Cut-out 'windows' can, like moon gates, give glimpses of the room or the landscape beyond.

A crisp, textured, beech hedge could be used to provide a lively and windproof surround for an immaculate vegetable garden, or, brown in winter, as a subtle backdrop for the dark stems of a frosty orchard, or as a link with the thatched roof of a summerhouse. Low box hedging can be used to make an attractive frame to borders or pools.

Planting: The success of a hedge largely depends on thorough preparation of the ground before planting: a well-prepared trench, forked over at the bottom, and with a rich mixture of topsoil and well-rotted compost, is ideal. Hedging can be obtained 'bare rooted' for winter planting; root balled, also ideal in winter; or container grown, which is suitable for planting throughout the year. Hedges can be planted as a single or double row, the latter establishing an effective barrier rather quicker but needing more plants. Spacing will vary with the species chosen.

Correct clipping is vital. Formal hedges should be clipped to a slight batter, so that they are slightly wider at the bottom than the top. This will enable adequate light and moisture to reach all the branches, and will ensure that the hedge grows evenly.

Contrasting & associating materials: Hedges are accommodating features, and do not set out to be stars in their own right. Formal hedging, however, associates especially well with crisp hard or soft landscape detail, and can look superb against sweeps of paving, gravel and manicured lawn.

CLIPPING A HEDGE
Clip hedges to a slight taper to allow light and air to reach all parts. This will ensure thick, even growth right down to ground level.

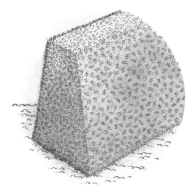

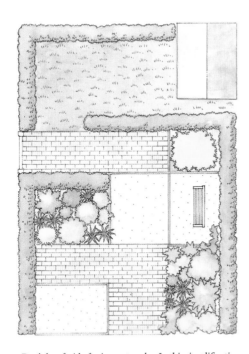

Don't be afraid of using rectangles. In this simplification of a modernist painting the hedging, planting and paving build up to make a subtle pattern.

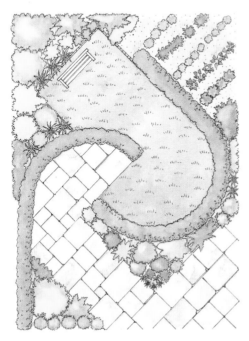

In a tiny garden, curving hedges break the sight lines, providing an air of mystery and surprise, as well as a feeling of space and movement.

Geometry is always an effective tool, and one of the garden designer's best allies. Planting hedges is often a far cheaper proposition than building expensive walls or dividers, and the solidity of this clipped box hedge creates a wonderful foil to the planting.

SUITABLE PLANTS FOR FORMAL HEDGES

HEDGING PLANT	PLANTING DISTANCES	CLIPPING REQUIREMENTS
Buxus sempervirens (box)	30cm (12in)	x 2–3 in growing season
Carpinus betulus (hornbeam)	60cm (24in)	x 1 mid to late summer
Crataegus monogyna (hawthorn)	45cm (18in)	x 2 in summer/autumn
x Cupressocyparis leylandii (Leyland cypress)	75cm (30in)	x 2–3 in growing season
Fagus sylvatica (beech)	60cm (24in)	x 1 in late summer
Ilex aquifolium (holly)	45cm (18in)	x 1 in late summer
Ligustrum (privet)	30cm (12in)	x 2–3 in growing season
Lonicera nitida	30cm (12in)	x 2–3 in growing season
Taxus baccata (yew)	60cm (24in)	x 2–3 in summer/autumn
Thuja plicata (Western red cedar)	60cm (24in)	x 2 in spring/early autumn

INFORMAL HEDGES

Characteristics: Informal hedges can be used in many different situations, but are particularly suited to country gardens, where they can provide privacy and shelter, as well as a link with the surrounding countryside. The character of the garden will be determined as much by how tightly these hedges are clipped as by the species used. An enormous range of shrubs is available, some with the added bonus of flowers and/or fruit, and here imagination can be brought into play. As well as obvious choices such as hazel, hedges of *Escallonia*, shrub roses, and forsythia can be used. Boundary hedges for country gardens are often mixed, including species such as hawthorn, field maple, hazel, elder, beech, dog rose, cherry, cornus, holly and wild viburnum. Some hedges are left unclipped and allowed to grow to their full height. Usually planted up with the larger shrubs, they require space to accommodate the mature plants. Suitable species are often evergreen, have a dense habit, the bonus of flower, and height

Forsythia is a striking shrub, both in terms of its structure and its dazzling colour. Its springtime yellow will beckon, or possibly deter, any caller, and such a hedge is virtually impenetrable. Such a vigorous hedge will need regular clipping and pruning to keep it under control, but where it is used as a positive statement it can be hard to beat.

enough to provide privacy and shelter. A distant division of the garden, planted with a mixture of rosemary, *Lavatera* and *Cotinus coggygria* 'Royal Purple' is simply delicious.

Uses: Informal hedges make fine boundaries that will blend in with the landscape beyond, but most are just as comfortable in an urban setting. They can be used to separate different parts of the garden – the kitchen garden from a flower garden or lawn; the orchard from a field – and some, if properly laid, will provide an impenetrable barrier to keep stock out or in.

Because of their ultimate size, unclipped hedges are usually best sited well away from the house, and can be used to make a link with other planting in the area. They can look fine in the country, but are also useful in an urban or suburban setting, where there is space, and can even be used as dividers.

This is a multi-layered hedge, the background providing a physical barrier, with the hydrangeas in front giving extra visual interest and softening the line of the former. The lower hedge and edging plants in the foreground complete the composition, giving it real depth. Such a combination avoids the austerity of planting a single species.

Planting: As for formal hedging, thorough preparation of the ground is essential, and the same planting directions should be followed. Most hedges of this kind will need regular pruning if they are to be kept tidy, or more radical cutting back and layering every few years to keep them growing thickly and to prevent them from becoming leggy and too high. Even unclipped hedges may need some thinning or pruning, according to the species selected.

Contrasting & associating materials: It is important to choose the plant species to suit the setting, but most hedges will associate well with other materials. The more informal of these hedges are ideal for pairing with rough grass, naturalized bulbs, and wild flowers. An orchard bounded by sprawling dog roses is a delight.

This is a delicious composition, with individual layers of different planting ranged formally in front of a delicate boundary of osiers. The planting embraces a number of different styles, with clipped lonicera giving way to a line of berberis and finally fastigiate conifers that echo the vertical line of the willow stems.

Even a hedge that falls beneath eye level provides an effective divider, encouraging movement through space between different 'rooms' within the garden.

SUITABLE PLANTS FOR INFORMAL HEDGES

HEDGING PLANT	PLANTING DISTANCES	CLIPPING REQUIREMENTS
Berberis darwinii	45cm (18in)	x 1 after flowering
Corylus avellana (hazel)	60cm (24in)	x 1 after flowering
Escallonia	45cm (18in)	x 1 after flowering; remove old wood
Forsythia x *intermedia* (forsythia)	45cm (18in)	x 1 after flowering; remove old wood
Fuchsia magellanica (fuchsia)	45cm (18in)	x 1 in spring; remove old wood
Lavandula (lavender)	30cm (12in)	x 1 after flowering
Pyracantha	60cm (24in)	x 1 in spring; remove weak and vigorous stems
Shrub roses	45cm (18in)	x 1 in spring; remove weak stems

PARTERRES, KNOTS & MAZES

Characteristics: Scrolled *parterres de broderie*, ornamental knots, and mazes have a long and distinguished history. Dating back many hundreds of years, they form important ingredients of many formal gardens.

Parterres and knots could be said to reflect the gardener's ultimate control of plant material, these intricate clipped patterns representing the dominion of mind over matter, as well as the sensitive manipulation of living material. Usually intended to be seen from above, their geometry never fails to catch the imagination. They were set pieces, intended for conversation and admiration; a far cry from the all-action role of the contemporary domestic garden. Traditionally, the spaces between the low hedges were filled with different coloured gravel, sand, coal and even glass, and only in comparatively recent times has planting been used.

Mazes are features on the grand scale, designed with a glorious sense of humour and the intention of making participants lose their way within the design. Hedges are normally used to outline the pattern, with yew as the first choice, and holly,

Although many parterres have historical connotations, they can be used in gardens of any period, whether classic or contemporary. They are also relatively fast to establish.

Here, the two colours of the different species of box have been trained to swoop over and under one another to great dramatic effect, forming a traditional knot pattern.

Mazes come in all shapes and sizes, and can be either formal or informal, but this pattern is gloriously organic in conception and outline. There is an enormous feeling of

rhythm and movement here which can be best appreciated from higher ground. The latter also allows a viewer to shout instructions to anyone lost inside!

which discourages cutting corners, running a close second. Hedges were not always above eye-level, and mazes can also be created from a pattern of paths, or simply mown out of a lawn, when willpower will play its part!

Uses: Although parterres were designed for grand gardens, the formula can easily be reworked in a simpler form to fit into a smaller plot. Small, ornamental beds of geometric design can be edged with low-growing plants and filled with a bold planting of a few or even a single species, or, in the traditional way, with different gravels. Bulbs followed by summer bedding is rigidly effective; box hedging filled with clipped santolina is stunning; and herbs and vegetables can also be used to form parterres. If you have the space, a hedged maze is always a possibility, but even a mown maze in the rougher grass of an orchard will give pleasure. Once you tire of it, you can change the pattern – or do away with it entirely.

Planting: Some of the best plants for edging parterres or knots include the small-leafed box, *Lonicera nitida*, *Berberis thunbergii* 'Atropurpurea Nana', and lavender. Fillers could include Dutch lavender, dwarf santolina, and bedding plants in a single colour.

Mazes can take the bolder material, such as yew, holly, beech and hornbeam. None of these is fussy about soil, but as for all hedges, good preparation is important. A maze is clipped in exactly the same way as for a normal hedge.

Contrasting & associating materials: Such features are essentially set pieces, and will look happiest within the geometry and with the natural materials of a traditional formal garden: natural stone, brick, gravel or grass paths, and sweeping lawns. However, there is no reason why such features should not be brought up-to-date, using crisp geometry and hi-tech materials. How about a maze in contrasting colours of Astroturf, or, even more off-beat, one constructed from acrylic mirror walls? Get out of that one!

Purple and grey is always a sound colour combination, especially when contained, as here, within a sweeping parterre edged with box and divided by carefully tended gravel paths. The secret of planting in such composition is to choose species that will not outstrip their allotted positions, thereby engulfing the dominant framework of hedging.

LARGE-SCALE AVENUES

This avenue, with its delicate cherry trees drawing the eye down towards the statue, would be relatively simple to duplicate in a medium-sized garden. Although the trees are attractively underplanted, this does not detract from the overall concept.

Characteristics: The purpose of an avenue is to heighten tension and lead the eye forward to focus on a major feature, usually the house but sometimes an incidental feature such as a pool, substantial garden building, or a fine view. An avenue on a grand scale requires space, integrity of design, and, above all, respect. This is not a device to be reproduced half-heartedly; it's all or nothing, and a row of scraggy cherries set in too small a plot in front of a pseudo-mansion lacks the style that an avenue deserves.

Avenues on this scale demand forest trees. Oak, chestnut, lime and beech can all be used, and their regular outlines will add to the drama. If stock are present, the lower branches will be automatically pruned, giving the trees an absolutely horizontal bottom edge. Fastigiate Lombardy poplars provide vertical emphasis, as well as tension at ground level, and form a dominant punctuation point from some distance away. They are also, unlike many other species, fast to establish, although relatively short-lived.

Uses: There are two major ways in which grand avenues are used: those flanking a driveway are primarily concerned with the approach to the house; others radiate away from the building, out into the landscape or towards a subsidiary feature. Apart from cross-axes, views to either side of an avenue should be discouraged, and the wide expanse of empty parkland through which such avenues often run, helps to add emphasis to the avenue itself.

Planting: A single avenue is superb, but a double avenue, where space permits, can look even more stunning. Avenues normally consist of repeat planting of the same species, and as a general rule, trees should be planted at least the distance of their eventual height away from a drive. Upright Lombardy poplars will be planted about 7m (20ft) apart while beech or chestnut will be spaced at about twice that distance. Stout stakes and tree guards are essential to prevent wind damage and possible attack by livestock.

Designers sometimes play around with false perspective, narrowing the avenue towards the focal point in order to achieve an impression of greater distance. While this just about works from the main viewpoint, it looks distinctly odd from the other end. Don't do it! Above all, remember that you are planting for future generations; this is a rare and wonderful thing to be doing today.

Contrasting & associating materials: Surrounding parkland and a gravel driveway are the least and the most that you will need; leave it at that!

Not all avenues need to be straight; here there is a real feeling of movement and mystery as the curving line of trees and mown grass draws you onwards. The rougher grass allowed to grow to its natural height provides just the right degree of delineation, but at the same time allows glimpses of the view to either side.

SMALL-SCALE AVENUES

Hostas are among the most architectural of garden plants. In this composition they are backed by a sombre avenue of young trees to provide great continuity. Notice how the white bench reflects the light back up the path; a darker colour would be far less effective.

Characteristics: The same principle of drawing the eye to a focal point (house, pool, statue, summerhouse, seat, or other garden feature) can be followed in a more intimate situation by using a regularly planted succession of clipped shrubs, or clipped or pleached small trees.

It is also essential that an avenue leads somewhere, and that once arrived at, the view back from a focal point is as strong as the view towards it. There is little point in arriving at a delightful summerhouse, only to turn round and have the eye led to the back of someone's garage – avenue or no avenue! Although usually planted, much the same effect can be achieved by using flanking posts and ropes, perhaps interspersed with small trees or lower planting.

Uses: Smaller avenues follow the same principles as large ones, but on a smaller scale. They often look best in a formal layout, and can be set within or contained by planting on either side, which will prevent the view from leaking out into other parts of the garden. An avenue can be a powerful device for drawing the eye away from a poor view, but the smaller the garden, the more careful you have to be to prevent it from dominating everything else.

Planting: Yews, clipped into a series of regular shapes, form some of the best small avenues, but some of the neater medium-height conifers also come into their own. Pleached trees are perfect for this scale of avenue, and can form a powerful and dramatic garden feature. Lime and hornbeam are ideal for this kind of high-level hedge, with their upper branches tied into wires to flank the avenue, and their stems left clean. They need careful pruning. Avenues, particularly those on a small-scale, can have a modern treatment as well as a traditional one. Try using architectural plants such as *Phormium*, *Yucca* or *Cordyline* to flank a crisp, contemporary path.

In all cases, straightforward but thorough soil preparation will be required. When planting, you should remember that the closer plants are positioned, the greater the feeling of tension will be.

PLEACHING TREES

Trees such as lime and hornbeam are ideal for pleaching. Carefully prune and train individual branches to horizontal wires stretched tightly between regularly-spaced posts.

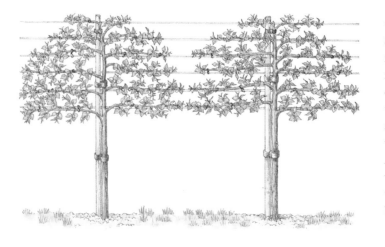

Contrasting & associating materials: Smaller avenues such as these relate more intimately to features and materials around them than avenues on a grander scale. A formal setting is usually best, but small-scale avenues set within subtly graded and colour-themed planting can be delightful. All will look superb in a situation where they are associated with traditional materials such as gravel, brick, grass, or natural stone paths.

MOVEABLE AVENUES

Instant colour, provided by cheerfully coloured annuals, can brighten an otherwise uninspiring scene. Without such a lift, the mid-green clipped box and dark brickwork of the steps, path and house in this composition would make a sombre scene.

Pleached trees provide high drama and considerable tension as you move between them. The narrower the avenue, the greater the visual restriction, which in turn accelerates the view and often the speed at which you negotiate the walk.

Characteristics: This is the smallest end of the avenue scale, and can work perfectly in even the tiniest garden. The rules are the same, though the lower the feature, the more the eye is drawn down to ground level, emphasizing the surrounding area. Moveable pots and containers trace their pedigree back to the 'Versailles' tubs used on the terraces and paths of the French palace. As with avenue trees, greater continuity and visual pulling power is achieved if the pots used are all of a kind, or at least used in repeated sequence. Planting is a question of choice. Clipped shapes engender greater formality than looser ones, but both are possible candidates; evergreens or evergreys can be used, or an entire range of flowering plants, from shrubs to annuals (remembering that cool colours are relaxing, and hot tones draw the eye); while tender exotics (moved indoors or discarded in winter) will give a tropical feel.

Uses: Moveable pots can be used to create mini avenues and vistas, even on a rotational basis, in different parts of the garden, and can form an integral part of the overall design, whether along paved or mown paths, flanking a lawn or terrace or reinforcing the line of a pergola. Planting can help to influence the formality or informality of the garden, while colours can be used to draw the eye through space. (Remember, if you mix colours in your avenue, to keep the hot tones, such as red, orange and yellow, closest to the main viewpoint, leaving cooler ones in the distance.)

Contrasting & associating materials: Bright, contemporary plastic or fibreglass pots look terrific in a modern setting; terracotta is comfortable nearly everywhere; wooden tubs can be either painted or treated with preservative; stone pots look best in a formal garden.

OVERHEAD
STRUCTURES

There is a huge range of pergolas from which to choose, whether you prefer the strict lines of an architectural style or the softness of a woodland walk. The latter provides a gentle walkway with the overhead canopy of foliage casting light shade across the path below.

While we accept that the floor and walls are essential parts of a garden, we often ignore the potential of the ceiling. In truth, the scope here is rather less obvious, but there are many overhead features – not the least of which are trees – that will help to contain and define the vertical space; useful tools for leading us through the composition, providing screening from intrusive views (or intrusive neighbours), and creating important focal points in their own right. Most of us are familiar with pergolas, arches, and overhead beams, but what of features such as arbours, fruit tunnels, and even awnings? All too often these major features are plonked down at random, or added as an afterthought, as a result of another impulse buying binge. To use them successfully, it is absolutely essential to think first what they can do for you, or for the garden as a whole, and work them into the overall plan. The prime rule is to understand just what each individual feature sets out to do; once that is established and a decision has been made, the rest will follow naturally.

All have long and distinguished pedigrees: pergolas were first used in Egypt as structures on which to grow vines and to provide shade; arches have been an integral part of the architectural and garden framework throughout history; arbours became retreats for meditation, relaxation privacy and love-making; and awnings, that cast great carpets of easily manipulated shade, go back to the very earliest times.

The secret to siting and using any features is to let the situation dictate the device – reinforcing the battle cry of the Modern Movement, 'form follows function!', which is the tenet of all good design. Pergolas, arches and tunnels will positively draw you through the space in a given direction. This, in turn, suggests the next rule: that these same features must lead somewhere. There is no point in designing and building a wonderful pergola that leads, as so often happens, straight to the compost heap! Equally unsatisfactory can be the habit of placing mirrors behind arches, or other features, in town gardens. To be successful this trickery needs careful manipulation, and considerable skill, but carried off with aplomb it can create a feeling of greater space. Design integrity is a delicate thing, and must be respected if the garden is not to end up a visually dishonest mess.

Another common denominator of pergolas, arches and tunnels is their ability to provide those essential ingredients, tension, mystery and surprise. As you approach, tension and expectation increase, and you wonder what lies beyond; as you emerge into a different part of the garden, surprise culminates in a release of tension.

Each feature handles this tension in a different way. An arch is quickly negotiated, and although a pergola takes longer, glimpses of the garden on either side will give a feeling of what lies around you. A tunnel is the most dramatic: a shadowy path that cocoons you in filtered sunlight, giving a tantalizing glimpse of what lies ahead, and into which you will burst on exit. With a device such as this, used to transport you from one room to another, it is essential that both ends are carefully positioned to ensure that the drama from either direction is worth the wait.

Static features like overheads and arbours attract in a different way, drawing you towards them. Overheads are essentially an extension of the house or other building, while arbours will be positioned further away, as a positive focal point. Both should reflect the overall style of the garden. Gloriously simple poles atop whitewashed columns and smothered in vines make a perfect Mediterranean overhead, but would look hopelessly out of place in the crisp architecturality of a European or American city, and arbours, too, should meet the same criteria. Too often you see over-designed structures clashing with their softer surroundings in the distant parts of the garden.

Awnings also need siting with care. Transient and colourful, they can be rolled out over a terrace, or simply cast over beams, or even the branches of a tree, to provide shade and shelter wherever it is needed. This kind of mobility in a feature usefully loosens up your mental attitudes, encouraging you to move freely about the garden to use different places to sit, dine or entertain.

Above all, it is of prime importance to choose and site major structures sympathetically within the garden as a whole, and to remember that understatement is invariably more successful than showing off – a philosophy that applies to gardens as well as to people! So, never pander to fashion or copy ideas for major features slavishly from a book; these will inevitably look awkward, whereas a comfortable and well-arranged garden with appropriate furniture will, like a comfortable living-room, fit your family like a glove.

As this structure is minimal, it barely breaks the view, which in turn contributes to its overall visual lightness whilst providing a gently dappled shade. Such an approach is in direct contrast to a heavier structure, where enclosure is the most important factor. Which type of structure you choose will depend on the character of the surrounding area.

METAL ARCHES

Characteristics: Metal has long been used for arches and pergolas, and its strength and durability make it an obvious choice. It is possible to achieve great delicacy of design, and you will see beautifully detailed and elaborate wrought iron designs in many historic gardens. The down side is the cost, and the need for a skilled metal worker to do the work.

Wrought iron can be worked by hand to virtually any pattern, whereas cast iron – popular with the Victorians as a cheap alternative – was only available in set patterns. Cast iron arches and pergolas can still be found at auction, but be careful as they are brittle, and if broken, virtually impossible to repair. Remarkably effective, simple designs can also be constructed from bent pipework, and I have seen superb purpose-built arches constructed from plumbing fittings. Oxidized copper, in particular, looks stunning, especially when covered with climbers. Bent mild steel rods, too, can be used, and will produce a very light effect. The structure is held together with galvanized wire, and if painted black will settle into the background. (Be sure to avoid the overworked thin white wire contraptions like the plague; they look dreadful.) Plastic-coated tubing is popular, has a long life, and comes in an alarming range of patterns, but the simpler shapes are acceptable, especially if you allow climbers to soften and detract from the structure.

Uses: Metal arches have a lightness and delicacy that makes them ideal hosts for delicate climbers that would be dominated by heavier structures.

Construction/erection: The older types usually had some kind of 'feet' that were surrounded by rammed soil or concreted in position. Concrete is the best fixing for modern arches.

Contrasting & associating materials: Depending on the style and materials chosen, they will easily blend into traditional or modern compositions.

Metal arches are simply vehicles for climbing plants, their delicacy of line and visual lightness allowing for minimal disruption to the overall scene. Hoops are often wired together, allowing climbers to scramble over the structure.

This simple hoop makes the most charming and informal arch, and is used to span this walkway, linking the two delightfully planted borders together. A timber arch would have been far too heavy here, whereas metal makes an ideal choice.

WOODEN ARCHES

Timber is the most versatile material at the garden designer's disposal, and this combination of a sturdy framework, laced with a delicate trellis, emphasizes the point perfectly. The picket gate cleverly echoes the curve of the arch.

Characteristics: Arches are strong vertical elements that demand attention, and will form important punctuation points in a garden. Timber is the commonest material used for their construction, and the easiest to handle. Styles vary enormously, from very basic affairs with just two uprights and a cross-member, to complex designs using all kinds of woodwork, struts and patterning. However, as with most things in the garden, the simpler things work best, and unless there is a very good reason for a complicated design (possibly to match the overall composition), arches are best kept simple. They should also be compatible with any adjoining divider or boundary, and either painted, or stained using a suitable non-toxic preservative.

Uses: Arches must be planned as an integral part of the garden design. They can be used to frame a path, link dividers, emphasize the entrance to a new garden room, or to act as a specific point of emphasis when entering the plot from the street.

Construction: This will be straightforward or complicated, according to the design. Simple arches can often be bought in kit form, and either concreted into the ground or set in spiked metal shoes. More complex designs are best built by a carpenter and assembled on site.

Contrasting & associating materials: Since an arch should reflect the overall style of the garden, it should blend into, rather than contrast with its immediate surroundings.

WOVEN ARCHES

Woven osiers can be used to create a structure that has far greater flexibility than the more usual split hazel wattles. This example sits comfortably among informal planting; climbers can be wired in position or allowed to twine naturally in with the weave.

Characteristics: Woven stems are a traditional garden material, and woven osiers (willow stems), reed or bamboo – all more flexible than the split hazel used for wattles – can be used to make arches and arbours to match the overall character of the garden. All these materials have a relatively short life, and you should expect them to last no more than eight or ten years. There is also the problem of squirrels which, in certain areas, seem to take delight in eating them. I have seen an entire arch, as well as woven figures, all made from osiers, disappear in this way in the space of two years.

Uses: Features such as these can be used in a wide range of settings, perhaps adjoining fencing made of similar material.

Construction: You will need a skilled craftsman, of which there are still a surprisingly large number. Weavers often display their work at county and rural craft shows. Features of this kind must be securely anchored to prevent them from being blown away in a high wind. The best method is to use bent wire spikes, which are much like tent pegs, threaded through the lower weave and driven firmly into the ground.

Contrasting & associating materials: Features made from these materials associate well with a wide range of other natural materials such as timber and stone, and look handsome set against and among planting. They go well with fencing made of the same material, or with woven garden furniture.

BRICK & STONE ARCHES

Characteristics: These are the most permanent members of the breed, almost always built as part of a boundary wall, major dividing wall, or adjoining a house or outbuilding. Where an arch pierces a wall, the solidity of the wall itself will give it additional punctuation power, while the addition of a gate or door will further increase the tension and expectancy of what lies beyond.

It is possible to mix brick and stone, and because brick is more easily worked than the latter, and forms a cleaner profile into which a door or gate frame can be fitted, you will often see a beautifully detailed brick arch set in a stone wall. The shape of a brick or stone arch can vary considerably; each – whether semicircular, pointed, flat or ogee – will contribute a different emphasis, and should always be determined by the overall style of the garden.

It is essential that a brick or stone arch is built as an integral part of the garden design. A poorly conceived arch of this kind can smack of the worst suburbanism. Arches built of a single thickness of brick, or of imitation stonework, tacked on to the house for no good reason, or self-consciously rising above a low boundary wall, perhaps with a flimsy wrought iron gate, should be avoided at all costs. Not only will these lack visual stability, but a misdirected knock with a heavily-laden wheelbarrow can often damage them beyond repair – perhaps the best fate!

Uses: As a major focal point and means of access through a boundary or internal dividing wall. Such arches demand attention, and positively draw both feet and eye towards them. This means that you can often highlight the area still further, perhaps by adding urns or fastigiate planting to either side.

Construction: As arches normally form part of a boundary or dividing wall, they will usually be built by a bricklayer or mason. The shape will be formed by a wooden template or turning piece, which is fixed into place to allow the brick or stonework to be built around it. Once the arch is completed, the turning piece will be removed. The wider the arch, the more complicated it is to construct.

Contrasting & associating materials: An arch must be entirely compatible with the wall in which it is set; both will be major elements in the garden as a whole. Brick walls and arches associate best with brick paving, stone with stone; both can be softened by planting. Where there is a mix of materials, such as brick and stone, then the dominant partner should link with similar materials.

Stone not only provides enormous structural and visual strength, but quickly acquires a patina of age that will settle it comfortably into the surrounding garden. This series of arches provides a powerful perspective that is effectively terminated by the carefully placed statue.

METAL PERGOLAS

There is a strong affinity between this metal pergola and the vine climbing over it as the twisted branches of the latter are virtually the same thickness as the smooth metal arches. Such a complementary visual dialogue forms the perfect garden feature.

Characteristics: The obvious advantages of metal over timber are its durability and strength. The strength of metal makes it possible to use thinner elements, so that the pergola can become a virtually invisible support for planting allowed to float over the surface.

Traditional examples, however, used a heavier gauge of metal, which was often worked into superb designs. Most were made of wrought iron, though some were cast and are therefore more brittle. I often find wonderful ones tucked away in neglected gardens, in various states of decay but always worth repairing.

One of the best contemporary examples I have seen was constructed from plumbing pipes and fittings. These allow a straightforward framework of uprights and overheads, with the added advantage that the overheads can readily be bent to form an arc. An excellent example of lateral thinking, in which the materials of one trade are used for quite a different discipline. I myself have built some wonderful hooped pergolas in large diameter pipework, painted in bright primary colours.

You can, of course, buy plastic-coated tubular metal for the purpose. While the simplest and most readily available shapes are just about acceptable, those that fall into the trap of 'design for design's sake'

certainly are not. No pergola, unless very carefully conceived and positioned, should aim to be a scene-stealer in its own right.

Uses: All pergolas are there for the purpose of supporting plants, and metal ones are less visually intrusive than timber ones.

Construction: Traditional examples often had a shoe, or bent metal section, incorporated at the bottom of each leg. This was firmly bedded in soil, or concreted into position, and provided virtually indestructible strength. Newer examples can be bought in kit form and slotted together. The vertical poles are either simply set in the ground (when they may not prove strong enough in a gale, once they are covered in plants), or concreted in. Fine mesh plastic can be stretched and tied over the whole structure to allow climbers to get an easy toe-hold.

Repairs to antique pergolas can often be carried out by a welder, and will probably need to be done on site.

Contrasting & associating materials: Traditional metal pergolas will blend into virtually any setting. Contemporary versions look great in the modern world. Modern plastic-coated affairs, which look pretty bland, look fine in bland gardens!

WOODEN PERGOLAS

The appearance of a timber pergola can be transformed by an application of paint. This eye-catching and vibrant structure, designed by Jill Billington, forms a striking focal point. The architectural line is emphasized by the crisp slate paving and the adjacent planting.

Characteristics: A pergola, a continuous series of arches, is essentially a vehicle for the plants grown over it and should always play second fiddle to the foliage and flowers of climbers and other associated planting. A pergola should be an integral part of the hard landscape framework of the garden, never an ostentatious addition. Timber (and less frequently, metal) is traditionally used, though you will also see brick or stone piers spanned by wooden beams. Many beautifully detailed examples of such pergolas can be found in historic gardens but never confuse impeccable detailing with fussy ornamentation; the two things are quite separate, and should remain so!

The flimsy rustic pergola of bark-covered larch poles is not only visually feeble, but will soon deteriorate; bark should always be removed from any structure as it traps water and encourages rot. However, this type of structure should not be confused with the round-pole pergolas and overhead features found throughout the Mediterranean, which are delightful, and very much part of a local vernacular style.

Uses: The purpose of a pergola is as a support which will allow climbing plants to be seen at their best, as well as a linking element between different parts of the garden.

Construction: Simplicity of design is important, and this means sound construction, using timber of generous proportions for both uprights and cross-beams. Hardwoods such as oak are especially suitable for outdoor wooden structures, and will last for many years, though softwoods, provided they are pressure-treated before purchase, or regularly treated with a non-toxic preservative, can also be used. Timber uprights can either be concreted into the ground, with the concrete brought just above ground level and slightly chamfered to shed water easily, or set into metal shoes that are driven into position before construction starts. Brick or stone piers will provide great durability and strength.

Planting will need unobtrusive support, particularly when training young plants, and wires can be neatly threaded through metal eyes screwed into the uprights and cross-beams.

Contrasting & associating materials: Timber associates well with brick or stone flooring, and brick or stone piers will allow the flooring material to be extended upwards, providing vertical continuity. A timber pergola will sit comfortably with timber trellis, which can be used to infill individual sections or to act as an extension, running out from the main structure and blending the line out into the wider garden.

Trellis was once a traditional material for constructing pergolas, giving the overall structure great visual lightness. It is less often seen in use today, but provided the timber is generously proportioned and regularly treated against rot, it can last for years.

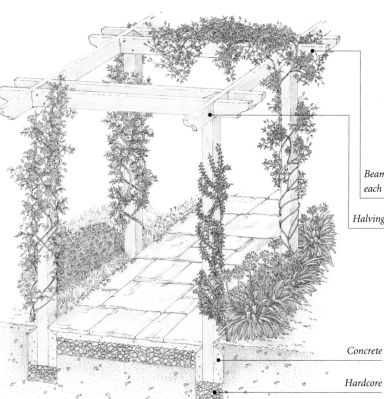

When is a pergola not a pergola? The dividing line between an archway or arbour can be a narrow one. This is a delightful and practical structure that could be used as a host for a wide range of climbing plants.

Beams may be shaped at each end or left square

Halving joints

DETAIL OF HALVING JOINTS

CONSTRUCTING A PERGOLA
Build pergolas using generously sized timbers to a design that is as sturdy as possible. Tie in climbers on to wires fixed both to the uprights and horizontals.

Concrete

Hardcore

TUNNELS

Characteristics: Tunnels seem inexplicably less popular than pergolas, yet they form delightful garden features and are not difficult to create. At their simplest, they need be little more than two parallel rows of hedge, trained to join at the top. They can be formed from yew or beech; from fruit trees, pleached limes and other trees; from willows plaited at the top; or, more informally, from trees planted in a narrow avenue with the canopy meeting at the top. Tunnels can be straight or curved, as space allows, and a curved tunnel will engender an enormous feeling of mystery as you wait for the view to open at the far end.

Tunnels can play host to a wide range of planting, and while there are few vegetables that could do the job, climbing beans work perfectly, adding their vibrant flowers to the architectural foliage. Metal hoops are visually undemanding and when covered, are virtually invisible, allowing the maximum amount of light to filter through the planting.

Metal hoops are again used as the underlying structure of this tunnel, but the trees have grown together to form a dimly lit passage that has slightly mysterious and even sombre overtones. The fine statue at the far end of the walk provides a focus and naturally draws you down towards the sunlight at the end of the tunnel.

Uses: Tunnels may be used in much the same way as pergolas, but must have somewhere positive to go. They are particularly successful in linking two different areas of the garden, but remember that the view back is as important as the way forward. A formally clipped hedge will relate best to a formal composition, while a tunnel of trees could be perfect in less formal parts of the garden.

Planting: In many instances you will need a framework on to which to train the plants that form the tunnel. For fruit trees, you will need either posts and wires, or, more traditionally, wrought iron hoops, over which the branches can be trained and tied. Limes and hornbeam can be tied into posts and wires, and the leaders trained over the top; willows are tied to stakes (also of willow), and carefully plaited as they grow. The stakes, incidentally, will almost always take root as well, and all species will need regular attention to keep the feature under control.

Contrasting & associating materials: This is a formal feature that looks best in an architectural garden setting or perhaps in a similarly conceived vegetable plot. A dark passageway of yew might be floored with pale gravel to reflect light, with a glimpse of white planting or sweeping lawns at the far end. A fruit tunnel, on the other hand, might be positioned to lead to an orchard or vegetable garden. Your own imagination is the best guide.

Freshly planted willow stems, even without their foliage in winter, can be used to create a fascinating pattern. The rhythm of the arching stems is echoed by the curve of the path that disappears with an air of mystery. Chipped bark provides a low-maintenance floor that perfectly complements the informal nature of the feature.

METAL ARBOURS

Where metal is of a sufficiently heavy gauge, rust can give it a warmth and patina that is rarely achieved by painting. This delightful fruit arbour provides a secret and shady retreat in which to relax on a hot summer's day.

Characteristics: Metal arbours are visually lighter than those built of timber, and if painted black are almost invisible from a distance. This gives them a great delicacy, in spite of their strength, and allows climbers virtually to float over the surface. There are fine old examples in many historic gardens, usually constructed from wrought iron, although the more brittle cast iron was sometimes employed in wonderful patterns. You can still obtain good wrought iron arbours, but they are generally made to order by craftsmen blacksmiths, and are expensive. Arbours made from plastic-coated metal or bent wire are also available, but tend to lack visual strength, even when covered by climbers.

I have designed arbours using heavy gauge galvanized piping, bent to shape and painted in glorious primary colours. These look terrific, and can form a powerful focal point, especially when positioned against a dark background of planting.

Uses: Metal arbours are used in exactly the same way as those made from timber.

Construction: Virtually all metal arbours, apart from the very simplest designs that can be constructed from bent steel rods or thick wire, are made by craftsmen. Most designs have legs that are bent over at the bottom to form an anchor set in a concrete foundation.

Contrasting & associating materials: Metal arbours blend well into a wide range of settings, but it is always important to respect the overall style of the garden.

Simplicity is all-important in a garden, and this delicious hoop frames the seat below and links the two clipped box balls on either side. The ivy smothering the pierced wall behind the bench has started to work its way over the arbour.

WOODEN ARBOURS

Timber is an infinitely flexible design material providing every opportunity to create something that is unique. Simple geometric shapes will be the most successful, and in this example the planting plays second fiddle to the structure itself.

Co-ordination within a composition is always important, and this seat has either been purpose built or impeccably chosen to blend with the rhythmically arched roof above. Fragrant planting such as jasmine or honeysuckle would be a natural choice for such a seat.

Characteristics: An arbour is a static feature, usually sited at some distance from the house and main terrace, which should provide an important focal point in the overall design of the garden. It will entice you to it, give vertical definition to the space, and act as host to fragrant climbing plants. The style in which it is built should relate directly to the rest of the garden, and an ideal position will be adjoining or surrounded by planting, which will naturally soften its outline.

Timber is a beautifully flexible material and there is virtually no limit to the design possibilities for a wooden arbour. Just bear in mind that simple structures are usually more successful than complicated ones. A number of off-the-peg designs are available, but these are often small and of dubious value; you can usually do far better yourself. Arbours need to be big enough to incorporate a table and chairs (though benches can be built into the framework to save space). Diminutive examples may look pretty, but will have little practical value as a sitting area.

Uses: An arbour will provide an informal sitting area, a place for relaxation, a place to pause at the end of a path, or, tucked away, a place to be 'happened' on. You must be led to it, rather than through it.

Construction: A wooden arbour will either be a straightforward carpentry job or a more complicated one, depending on its design. Hardwood, or pre-treated softwood can be used, and posts should be generous in their dimensions: at least 10cm (4in) square, and often more. They should be set in concrete foundations or adjustable shoes driven into the ground. The sides can be left open, or filled with one of the many designs of trellis available, which will provide support for climbers. The roof will be an open structure, and although timber can be used for this in a variety of ways, wrought iron will also make an excellent and delicate ceiling. The floor can be formed from one of a whole range of surfaces, from grass to brick paving, though hard materials provide a better all-weather surface.

Contrasting & associating materials: Arbours are adaptable, and should reflect the style and materials used in their immediate surroundings. Heavy, rustic timbers might be used in a woodland area, or crisply sawn and planed boards in a more contemporary situation. Floor paving should follow suit.

OVERHEAD BEAMS

Characteristics: Overhead beams help to define the space beneath them, and by extending the line of a house or other building out into the garden or landscape, visually and physically help to tie the two elements together. Overheads are normally made of timber, and link best with a timber building; however, colour can also be used to reinforce it. They should be left as an open structure; any roofing, whether of clear plastic or any other material, will simply collect debris, and sound like thunder in any but the lightest shower. Overheads are found, in different vernacular forms, all over the world: from rough-hewn timbers on the Indian sub-continent to crisp sawn and planed boards on the west coast of America.

Uses: As well as the uses mentioned above, overheads can also break a view providing privacy from the upstairs windows of neighbouring properties, give dappled shade, and play host not only to a child's swing, but also to fragrant climbing plants or hanging plant containers.

Although overhead beams are the simplest of structures, they immediately succeed in defining the vertical space beneath them, providing an informal ceiling. Climbers, in this case wisteria, can be used to soften the line and cast a dappled shade beneath.

OVERHEAD BEAMS
Either run overhead beams out from the house or from a free-standing wall. Use 220 × 50mm (9 × 2in) timber joists, set in hangers off the wall and supported by scaffolding poles at their extremities.

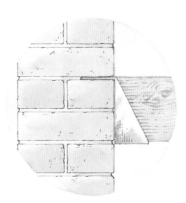

JOIST HANGER
Either build joist hangers into a new wall, or insert them into an existing one.

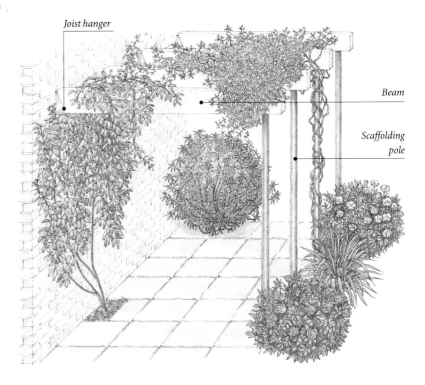

Joist hanger

Beam

Scaffolding pole

Construction: Timber can be worked in many ways, and overheads should be used to match the style of the adjoining architecture. As a general rule, the simpler the construction the better, and beams usually look best with square cut ends rather than being nosed off at an angle or cut into complicated patterns.

Beams are usually fitted to the house with joist hangers, and supported at the other end by a cross beam fixed to timber uprights or screwed to metal poles (which often look best painted black). Uprights should be firmly concreted into the ground, and timber should be pre-treated against rot, or painted. An ample depth of topsoil should be left around the uprights to accept climbing plants, and, depending on the planting, uprights and beams may need wires run through metal eyes so that climbers can be tied in.

Contrasting & associating materials: Overhead beams should associate with the architecture and garden they adjoin. Crisply sawn timbers will look perfect with geometric paving, bold railway sleepers and gravel. Rough hewn beams will sit comfortably with more relaxed, natural and informal surfaces.

ATTACHING POLES TO BEAMS
Fit scaffolding poles with a timber dowel before using a double-ended screw to fix the latter into the beam.

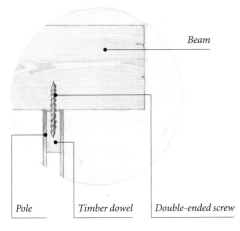

Beam

Pole   Timber dowel   Double-ended screw

AWNINGS

Characteristics: Awnings can be reeled out from fittings attached to the house, or simply draped over a framework of overhead beams and roughly fixed in position to prevent them blowing off in the wind. At their most basic, and mobile, they can be formed from a sheet thrown over a frame or the branches of a tree. Fabric can be waterproofed canvas or polyesters, both of which come in a vast range of colours, or woven matting, easily purchased from a store or local craftsperson. Plain colours are often the most successful, and in a sophisticated situation the colour or pattern of the awning and outside cushions can be chosen to echo the interior design of the house. Although white can be elegant, it may be rather glaring in strong sunlight and it also shows dirt easily. Thin muslin, though, will filter the sunlight, producing near magical conditions beneath its shade, and it can be tied into wonderful swagged tents to create a particular style or atmosphere. The disadvantage is that being such a fine fabric, it has a relatively short life.

Uses: The purpose of an awning is to cast shade, either to provide agreeable sitting conditions for people, or to prevent fabrics and furniture inside the house from bleaching in sunlight. They can also be used in a mobile and delightfully informal way to provide an enticing oasis of shade anywhere in the garden.

Construction: Awnings can be bought in kit form, complete within a boxed framework of variable size that can be bolted into position. Alternatively, fabric can be cut to size, finished off if there are raw edges, and casually slung over beams or a more informal structure in the garden.

Contrasting & associating materials: Awnings will have a natural affinity with other fabrics in the garden or in the adjoining house. They can also be used to match or contrast with the paintwork, paving, or even plants; a pale fabric, for example, would make an effective contrast with darker paintwork on the walls.

In this austere but superbly architectural situation the awning introduces attractive contrasting elements of softness and delicacy. The use of finer fabrics for awnings tends to filter the sunlight slightly rather than blocking it out entirely, and can thereby look more attractive than heavier materials.

MAJOR
FEATURES

Focal points come in all shapes and sizes, and this one is a real scene stealer. Not only does it stand out in sharp relief against the background but it is also in possession of a roof with a strong vertical emphasis that draws the eye and demands attention.

A garden without features of any kind is a clean canvas; to bring such a garden to life requires careful planning, to reflect the personalities and needs of those who use it. The planning will initially produce a basic structure or framework, consisting of boundaries, surfacing of various kinds, and possible ceiling treatments in the form of overheads. Once the framework has been established, features, which will almost certainly become important focal points, can be chosen and positioned.

When you start to plan a garden it is essential to compile a list of all the things that you like and dislike, throwing this open to the whole family. Some items, such as sheds and greenhouses, will be purely functional; others, such as water features, rock gardens or raised beds, will be decorative; some, such as play equipment or a swimming pool, will provide a specific activity. Some may even serve a dual purpose: a treehouse for play will also attract the eye upwards, and a gazebo, as well as providing somewhere to admire the view, will provide a decorative feature.

All major features, however, will play an important visual role, drawing the eye, and this in turn means that they will need to be positioned with care, so that they create an overall pattern that is easy to live with in visual terms, but is at the same time practical.

Obviously, the larger the garden, the more scope there is for focal points of this kind, particularly if the area has been divided into separate spaces, each with its own identity. A garden full of major features would inevitably look 'busy', but the total number is not important; what is important is to ensure that only a few are visible at any one time.

There are almost unlimited ways in which a feature can be built or interpreted, but it is important that the overall style of the composition is respected, and that the siting of the item is chosen with care. To position an informal, irregularly shaped pool in a formal terrace would simply look incongruous, as would a traditional summerhouse placed in an *avant garde* design that used modern materials and crisp patterning.

It is also possible to highlight and manipulate a major feature by the way it is sited within the garden. A circular pool and fountain can be given added emphasis by the smooth plane of surrounding lawns, and this can be heightened yet further by a ring of dark yew hedging and carefully chosen statuary. The same feature without this drama would not be insignificant, but it would certainly be less telling.

The siting of features is largely to do with the balance of the garden as a whole, and the easiest way to understand this is to imagine a pair of scales. A formal design would use weights of equal size, balanced at equal distances from the fulcrum (for example, matching pools or bridges at either end or side of the garden), whereas an asymmetric design would use unequal weights balanced at unequal distances from the fulcrum (for example, a group of trees towards the bottom of a garden on one side, balancing the visual weight of a large summerhouse on the other).

In general terms, the key to choosing and using features is to remember that the areas closest to the house are naturally more architectural or formal than those farther away, where the character of the design can become softer and looser. Whereas crisp built-in seating, a formal pool, or rectangular raised beds will sit comfortably nearer the house, a winding stream, informal pool, or treehouse will be right for the farther parts of the garden.

The position of some features will, however, be determined by their use: it makes sense to site a barbecue close to the kitchen, and a play area in view of the house; a rock garden or greenhouse will benefit from an open, sunny aspect, while a shed is probably best sited further away, and may well need screening. The siting of others may be affected by climate: a swimming pool that is used all year round in a warmer climate, for example, may be best sited near the house; in a temperate climate, where it is used for only part of the year, this may be better set in a sheltered position in a farther area of the garden.

Certain features will also be suggested by the topography of the site. A sloping garden will lend itself to water, in the form of streams, cascades and pools. You can achieve all these things on a flat site, but a dramatic change of level will not only make things easier in constructional terms, but will also look more natural. Rock gardens or rocky outcrops also fit well into sloping ground, while a swimming pool sited below a diving rock has the most wonderful charisma. Flat gardens, on the other hand, are perfect for expansive pools that set up ever-changing reflections, and the dynamics of a bridge spanning a particular point, will bring the third dimension into play.

You, or your contractor, will need to check local regulations on siting and using a swimming pool, as well as soil conditions, water table, access to power, water and drainage.

Before you start on the design, and certainly before you build the garden, it is also important to work out just how much maintenance you are prepared to undertake. Some features need an inordinate amount of work to maintain them. Rock gardens are generally time-consuming, whereas raised beds, that bring the working surface up to a manageable height, make life a good deal easier. Swimming pools are notoriously labour intensive, whereas a bog garden, with its lush, bold planting, can virtually look after itself.

Remember, too, that a garden may well change over the years, as patterns of life alter, and families grow and move on. Such changes may be the result of your spending either less or more time looking after the garden. Features will come and go, be modified, or perhaps fall into decay. In the case of a pool becoming a boggy area, this might be the basis of an entirely new and unforeseen use.

Some places are special, and because of that become natural focal points. The crisp decking and chairs used in this design introduce a successful architectural element into an otherwise soft composition, and the adjacent water sets up a series of reflections.

FORMAL PONDS

Classical formality usually relies on repetitive geometry, which can be static, but the introduction of water introduces both movement and a delicate sound.

Characteristics: Formality in a garden is a powerful element, often producing a rigid and balanced framework that benefits from softening. This can be done in a number of ways: planting is an obvious choice, but water, with its changing moods, reflections and movement can be another perfect team player. Great gardens using water in a formal way are found throughout the world, from the majestic splendour of the great Italian Renaissance compositions, to the Moorish courts of the Alhambra. In hot climates water provides a cooling influence and reflections under wide skies, whereas in the softness of a temperate climate it gives a feeling of tranquillity. Even on a small scale a formal pool, if correctly conceived and sited, can introduce these same elements.

Formal pools look their best set within the geometry of a terrace close to a building, or within a balanced framework of lawns and hedges in the middle or more distant parts of the garden. Near the house, a pool will normally be designed into the hard landscape framework of a terrace, often in a rectangular shape as part of the overall paving pattern. In lawns and planted areas, pools may be edged with stone, set with statuary, and furnished with exquisite fountains. Here, the shape may be either rectangular or circular rather than free-form curves, and this can be reflected in the planting of surrounding hedges or borders.

One of the most important uses of water is to introduce movement into an otherwise static design. The architect Sir Edwin Lutyens was a master of formality, and a genius with water, building superbly detailed pools, falls and chambers. By looking at his work you can start to understand the subtlety and importance of using such an element within a garden design. Although formality is often associated with traditional gardens, hi-tech and contemporary designs can use water in astonishing ways, contained within polished steel, fibreglass or sealed concrete shells.

Uses: Formal pools can be used both as a softening element within a strongly architectural area, as a focal point, or as a link between different parts of

A small water feature becomes more effective if it is raised closer to eye level. The brick coping, with its beautifully detailed corner, is at the perfect height for sitting.

Formality is as pertinent in a contemporary setting as a traditional one. This composition of great strength and tranquillity proves that garden design can work as pure art.

the garden. Changes of level can provide opportunities for split-level pools, water cascades, or water staircases to link adjoining areas. If the water is moving, it will have an extraordinary influence in drawing you through the space; an effect that a row of fountains set down the length of a long pool will also have.

Construction: Many historic pools were built of stone set in watertight clay. Later, concrete replaced clay, but there were inevitable problems with settlement cracks and leakage. Today, different grades of butyl rubber, plastic and polyester laminates are used to form virtually indestructible liners.

Pools can be made shallow enough to form stairs or falls, or deep enough to support fish and planting. As a general rule, 600mm (2ft) is ample for domestic pools, and plants that enjoy shallow conditions can be positioned on marginal shelves. Levels must be carefully worked out and excavations given a smooth profile, with sharp stones removed and a base layer of damp sand laid to act as a cushion for the liner.

A simple formula for working out the size of liner you need, is to add twice the maximum depth to the maximum length and width of the pool. The liner is then positioned and loosely anchored around the edge of the pool with bricks or coping, and water is run in until the liner is moulded into shape. Once the water has nearly reached the top of the excavation, it can be trimmed to shape, nicked to make it lie flat around any curves, and the coping laid to overhang the water and create a line of shadow. With rectangular pools there is always a tendency for the liner to pucker in the corners. Certain manufacturers will 'tailor' the liner by welding the sides and bottom, so that it fits the excavation exactly. Coping round the pool should match materials used elsewhere in the garden, and if you are thinking of using statuary, it, too, must be chosen and positioned with great care to match the mood of the overall composition. Fountains look fine in a formal pool, and if moving water

is required, this will probably be powered by submersible pumps, and power will have to be laid to the pool to cater for this.

Contrasting & associating materials: Water is an adaptable element, and will blend into the widest possible range of settings and materials, both traditional and contemporary.

CONSTRUCTING A POND

Set out circular pools to a specific series of radii. Excavate the ground to a depth of 225mm (9in) for the marginal shelf, before digging to the full depth of 450mm (18in) being careful to slightly angle the sides. After removing any sharp stones, add a base layer of damp sand or geo-textile to act as a cushion under the liner.

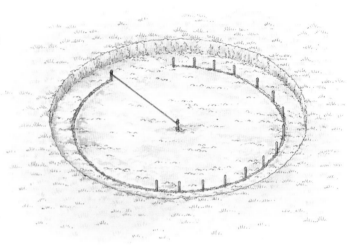

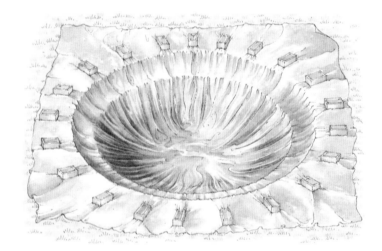

Once the excavation is complete, roughly place the liner into position and anchor it with bricks. When the water is run in, it will mould the liner to shape.

HARD EDGING FOR A LINER POND

Bricks set on edge in mortar just below the level of the surrounding turf form a crisp coping.

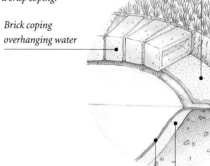

Mortar

Brick coping overhanging water

Butyl liner   Sand   Soil

INFORMAL PONDS

Ideally, it should be impossible to tell that an informal pond has been artificially created. This is easier to achieve if the setting is large enough to handle a composition of adequate size and conviction. A change of level also adds immeasurably to any such situation, providing the bonuses of sound and movement to the scheme.

Characteristics: While formal pools demand an architectural treatment, their informal counterparts, more fluid in shape, will blend into the farther parts of the garden, relating to lawns and borders with strong flowing curves, which in turn set up a real feeling of space and movement.

The larger the pool, the more generous associating features can be. A simple bench and sitting area will probably look just right by a small pool. However, on the banks of a large area of water that is verging on being a lake, a generous summerhouse, boathouse or other major feature would look in perfect scale.

Classical fountains and statuary are difficult to use successfully in an informal pool, but planting can provide a wonderful extra dimension, both in the water and surrounding the feature, blending it into the wider garden. Moisture-loving plants, with their bold foliage, are among the most handsome on the garden designer's palette. All water benefits from an open position that is not overhung by too many trees.

Uses: Informal pools are wonderfully versatile in their uses: they are a haven for wildlife of all kinds; they set up reflections that mirror the changing moods of the surrounding composition and the sky above; they act as major focal points at any time of the year. Any area of open water can be a hazard to young children, who should always be supervised when near it, but pools can provide hours of fascination and learning for youngsters. If you are lucky enough to have a lake, then the pleasures of boating and simply messing about on the water will be quite irresistible.

Construction: The curves of an informal pool should be laid out with great care. The disastrous technique, encouraged in so many gardening books, of casting a hosepipe on the ground, kicking it about, and then cutting out the shape, should be avoided at all costs; it simply produces a convoluted series of wiggles that are hard on the eye and a chore to maintain. Instead, observe how nature handles curves, particularly in a watery situation, and do the same: the shapes will always be positive, generous and gentle. You can achieve this best by drawing the curves with a pair of compasses on the drawing board, sweeping one bold curve into the next, and then setting these out in the garden by swinging a line from the radii involved.

Like formal pools, the majority of informal pools are lined with butyl rubber or laminated plastic. In some situations, coping will be unnecessary: a grassy bank, poolside planting, cobble and boulder beach or boggy area could all be created to blend the water softly into its surroundings.

Contrasting & associating materials: Lawns, planting, and beaches of various kinds are the perfect counterpoints to informal water. Coping stones or coping brick should almost certainly match materials used elsewhere in the garden. Decking looks superb, as do the more relaxed forms of paving such as random rectangular paving, granite setts and brick.

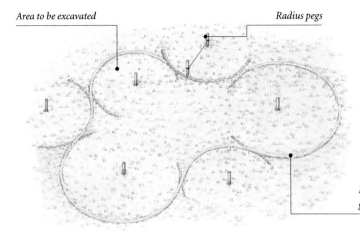

Area to be excavated — Radius pegs

MARKING OUT AN INFORMAL POOL

Radii can be of any size, but the more generous the better, with one curve running smoothly into the next. When designing a pool remember that a marginal shelf will be approximately 225mm (9in) wide and deep, which will reduce the area of deeper water.

Radiused curves scored on to grass or marked out with sand

MARGINAL PLANTING AT THE EDGE OF A POND

To form a bog garden, or damp area at the edge of a pond, allow water to seep into an adjoining bed that is contained by a continuation of the butyl liner.

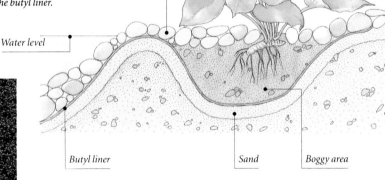

Loose cobble beach allowing seepage

Water level

Butyl liner — Sand — Boggy area

This is a perfect and fascinating example of how an essentially formal pattern can be softened by planting. While the trickle of water introduces movement, the Pachysandra *overhanging the water transforms a simple composition into something more mysterious.*

INFORMAL EDGING FOR A LINER POND

An informal 'beach' can be formed with loose cobbles set on a gently sloping shelf around the edge of the pool.

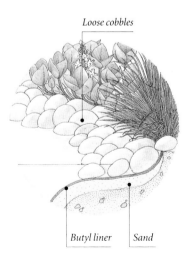

Loose cobbles

Butyl liner — Sand

WOODEN BRIDGES

There is a narrow line between the production of design for design's sake and the creation of a work of art. I place this bridge in the latter category, with its highly stylized pattern *and Japanese overtones, and its narrow approach that guides you strictly down a specific route. The planting provides the perfect counterpoint to this formal design.*

can while away endless hours. Once again, the style of the bridge should suit the underlying design of the garden. Bridges are dramatic features in themselves, but the drama is often overdone, with bright red Japanese designs placed in quiet country gardens, or hideously overworked and garishly white structures in quite ordinary situations. Never be tempted into design for design's sake of this kind; forget the glossy manufacturers' catalogues with their horrendous prices; instead, look around you at vernacular styles, and remember back to the simple designs you saw as a child. Then get a skilled local craftsman to use his commonsense and knowledge to build you a bridge; the results should be more than worthwhile.

Uses: Bridges are quite simply paths across water and otherwise impassable areas, but they are also important directional tools. Water, even at its shallowest, is a real deterrent to access, and a

Characteristics: Timber is one of the most adaptable of materials, and can be considered for a variety of uses in the garden and to create virtually any style, shape or pattern. When it is used for bridges, the advantages are obvious: you can build structures from the simplest planks laid across a brook, to a complex structure that soars over a stream or inlet.

Bridges are one of the ultimate tension points, as they lead you across what is essentially an alien element at a specific point in the composition. This can set up all kinds of interesting possibilities, from the excitement of wobbling across logs or railway sleepers set over a boggy area, to the wistful enjoyment of leaning over the solid handrail of a sturdy bridge to enjoy the sight and sound of water sliding underneath.

Bridges are rarely devices to be hurried across, and the broader and more generous they are, the more pleasurable the experience. Children adore them, which is the best justification for sound construction and safety; the fun of floating 'Pooh sticks', or bombing leaves with anything to hand,

Is this the path to a secret garden over a small stream that is full of movement and trout for tickling? The bridge, constructed from two railway sleepers and bordered with *sensibly sturdy handrails, is impeccably simple and unsophisticated. The temptation to walk across this bridge and down the flower-edged path is almost irresistible.*

well-sited bridge can open up a whole new area of garden – on an island, or the farther side of a stream. There are other situations, apart from crossing water, where a bridge might span a lane or deep gully in a woodland area. On a smaller scale, even a simple structure over a garden pool can dramatically influence the way in which you move around the garden.

Construction: Bridges should be built to a scale appropriate for the use they can expect: whether for pedestrians, animals, vehicles, or perhaps all three. Their use and situation will often determine the final shape and therefore the skills, and the expense, involved. A large span over deep water or across a rocky gully may well need to be arched for strength, fitted with robust hand rails for safety, and bolted down to secure concrete foundations on either side; this is an advanced joinery project that will probably require help from a professional. A bridge forming a mere continuation of a track over a rill might simply consist of logs cut to length, roughly shaped, and securely bedded on either bank. Between these two extremes lies a wealth of sensible designs that can be carried out by most competent carpenters. Many bridge projects use similar techniques to decks, and the latter can often be adapted or extended to cross water in the most imaginative ways.

Hardwood handrails are usually more handsome, and certainly more durable, than softwood rails, and they can be worked in a variety of fascinating patterns. Any timber, hard or soft, will need to be initially and regularly treated to withstand rot.

Contrasting & associating materials: This will depend on the situation (timber bridges could be an extension of a timber deck, a gentle continuation of an informal path through a woodland, or a crisp contrast to pale precast paving), but the right or wrong design decision can make or mar a composition. In other words, use your head and don't get seduced by silly pictures in glossy magazines.

METAL BRIDGES

Metal can be both incredibly strong and visually light, and it can be used to span greater distances than would be possible using timber. This delicate tracery, with its braced handrails, allows the view to run through the bridge, and the sweeping line introduces a feeling of movement. The whole construction has been painted in the ideal colour, black.

Characteristics: Metal has a strength and delicacy that sets it apart from other materials. These characteristics make it suitable for large spans which can float over water, and for a wide range of styles, both traditional and contemporary. Metal is often used as a substructure for timber, with the metal providing strength for the main frame, and timber being used for the walkway and rails.

You can see fine examples of cast iron bridges in many historical gardens, and since the full potential of the material took some time to be realised, the earliest sometimes have wood-working joints. The most sophisticated bridges, used in grand gardens with other major features, are suspension bridges, where delicacy of design is combined with great strength.

Contemporary bridges are usually built from a variety of steel, wire and mesh, and since most metal, apart from stainless steel, is painted, this allows a link to be made with colours used elsewhere in the garden. As a general landscape colour, however, black is hard to beat, and will blend into virtually any background; white is far too visually demanding, and should be used with extreme circumspection.

Uses: As metal is immensely strong, these bridges can be used to span distances where timber or stone would fail, and to cater for even the heaviest vehicles. However, metal can also be used to construct the most exquisite and charming small pedestrian bridges.

Construction: Metal is a specialist material, and bridges are almost invariably designed by experts and fabricated off-site, before being assembled in the garden.

Contrasting & associating materials: The materials used for the bridge should match those of the surrounding landscape. A steel bridge will perfectly complement a steel and glass building, while a subtly arched wrought or cast iron structure could soar between lawns or woodland. Surrounding hard landscape materials should follow the same philosophy.

STONE BRIDGES

The simplest of bridges can be formed using roughly hewn slabs of natural stone; once positioned, these will remain permanently in position. The staggered pattern shown here provides an interesting variation on a straight crossing.

Characteristics: As with a timber bridge, the style of a stone bridge can be simple or complicated: from a straightforward slab laid over a garden pool or brook, to the full-blown splendour of a Palladian masterpiece spanning a lake. The differences are obvious, both in situation and cost. Stone is not only more expensive, but both visually and physically harder than timber. As with any structure, the type and colour of stone used, and the building style, needs to blend into the overall setting.

Uses: Stone is one of the strongest and most durable materials you can use in the garden. It is also the heaviest, and so its first resting place will almost certainly be its last. In other words, you need to get it sited right first time! Stone bridges are suitable for all kinds of access, but particularly where the bridge is to carry heavy loads and support heavy wear.

Construction: This will again depend on the complexity of the project. A sizeable slab of stone can be manhandled into position with the help of many bodies and basic tools. It will probably not need foundations or shaping in any way. A full-blown arch, on the other hand, will need comprehensive footings and a degree of skilled labour.

Contrasting & associating materials: Stone is very much a generic material, and looks best, not in isolation, but when it is used across the garden. A similar stone should be used throughout, and the style should echo the overall tone of the background composition. When mellowed, stone has the ability to complement nearly everything around it: paving, planting, lawns, water and woodland.

CONSTRUCTING STEPPING STONES ACROSS A POND

To ensure that the stepping stones are stable, build the piers on a foundation of 75mm (3in) smoothly trowelled concrete over a 150mm (6in) layer of hardcore. Set the slabs to just above water level, overlapping the piers.

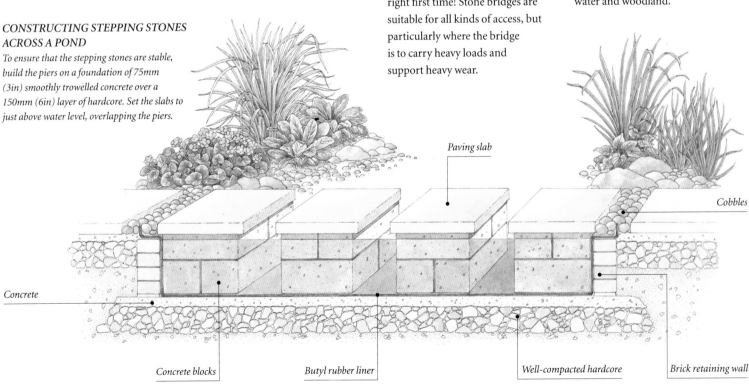

Paving slab

Cobbles

Concrete

Concrete blocks

Butyl rubber liner

Well-compacted hardcore

Brick retaining wall

Stepping stones make the ideal crossing for a small pool and can easily be set on piers made from concrete blocks or bricks. As a sensible precaution, use textured slabs to provide a good grip; these should be constructed to overhang the supporting piers by about 50mm (2in). The piers themselves may be camouflaged by being painted black.

SMALL WATER FEATURES

Even the smallest pool can introduce both a cooling influence and a feeling of movement. The paving is an extraordinary, but successful, combination of concrete and broken plates, which contrasts effectively with the vibrant colours of the adjacent planting.

Characteristics: There are situations in which it may not be possible or desirable to have a large or even moderately-sized pool: the garden may be tiny; shade may be a problem; a wide expanse of water could be a hazard to young children. There are, however, a range of features that are both safe for children, and can be tailored to fit the smallest areas. Some, such as a millstone or boulder fountain, rely on re-circulated water being pumped up and over the surface from a sump concealed beneath. Others consist of a bowl or series of bowls that are fitted to a wall, with water spilling from one to the next, and eventually dropping to a small raised pool.

A superb contemporary feature known as a Kügel consists of a polished sphere of granite that floats on low-pressure jets of water just clear of a matching cup, also made of granite. The feature is fitted with solenoids that control the water jets, turning the ball slowly one way and then another, allowing sunlight to sparkle off the surface. It is perfectly safe and irresistible to even the smallest children, whose tiny fingers cannot be trapped beneath the revolving surface.

Water will help to cool an area on the hottest summer's day, but it is the sight and sound of water that is the most important reason for finding a place for it in a garden. Water is one of the most valuable elements in helping to relieve stress, and watching an ever-changing cascade or a bubble jet fountain can evoke an extraordinary feeling of peace.

Uses: Small water features can of course be used where space is at a premium, but can also provide a point of emphasis in many parts of the garden. Because of their intimate scale, they often look best and feel

WATER FEATURE WITH BOULDERS

To create this feature, set a large water tank on level ground. Build piers inside the tank to support the boulders, filling the spaces around them with smaller smooth stones. Position a submersible pump in the base of the tank to send water in two directions: straight up through a drilled boulder, and out of the tank and through another drilled boulder to spray water back into the tank below. Use valves to control the flow.

There are endless variations on this theme where water can be pumped over and through drilled rocks or millstones.

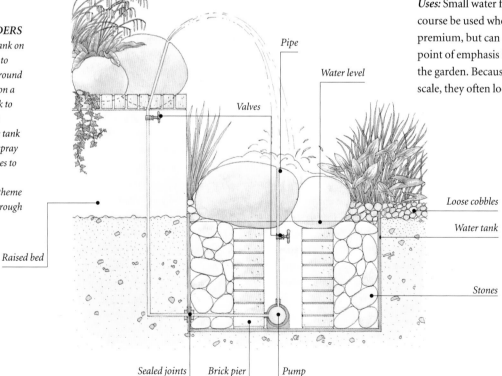

Pipe

Water level

Valves

Raised bed

Loose cobbles

Water tank

Stones

Sealed joints   Brick pier   Pump

Good humour is an essential part of successful garden design, and while this is a highly individualistic statement it is also successful. The contrast of materials and colours is particularly telling, and the sound effects must be delightful.

most comfortable set within or close by a sitting area, and are often most telling when positioned so that they can be seen from within the house. Apart from their obvious visual and audible qualities, they will also provide a valuable source of water for birds, butterflies and bees.

Construction: Almost all these features use re-circulated water fed from a submersible pump. The millstone, or its derivative, is usually set on piers built up within a tank and level with its top, the pump is placed on the bottom, the area between the top of the tank and the stone is covered with a metal mesh concealed with loose cobbles and boulders, and the tank is then filled with water. A simple dipstick will tell you when to top the feature up; it is

surprising how much evaporation can take place on a hot summer's day.

Wall plaques, bowls, and similar water features are usually set into the surface of the wall and held in position with metal ties, along with the associated plumbing.

Contrasting & associating materials: All these features are highly individualistic and should be chosen carefully to suit their surroundings. A series of cast stone wall cascades might be appropriate for a formal area or chic town garden, whereas a large boulder, drilled through the middle and spilling water on to a bed of cobbles would suit a less formal situation. A contemporary Kügel would fit best in a modern setting, whereas a millstone would look superb in an old courtyard.

The symbolism of Japanese gardens is both delicate and difficult to reproduce as each component has its own special significance. However, when handled correctly, the results can be stunning, with a great sense of permanence and stability.

FOUNTAINS

There is a great deal of drama and movement in this design, both in the fountain that breaks the surface of the spa bath, and in the soaring steps that burst right through the wall and lead into the garden beyond. The details shown here are adjacent to a swimming pool, resulting in a composition that is entirely complementary

Characteristics: Fountains have been around for centuries, and many of the oldest classical gardens used them in abundance. You have only to visit the great Renaissance gardens of Italy to see fountains in all their magnificent glory, drama and raw power. The secret of their success lies in their relationship to the surrounding garden, and this all depends on scale. Whereas a large garden can accommodate a sizeable pool complete with a correspondingly large fountain, problems arise in small gardens when people insist on a soaring jet that both looks ostentatious and can quickly drain the pool dry – the slightest breeze will blow the water out of the area.

In a formal situation, a fountain can make the most telling focal point at the end of a vista, and fountains arching in from the sides, or set in line down the middle, will lead the eye down the length of a long stretch of water. In an asymmetric design, a fountain can be offset, to balance another feature in a different part of the garden. The height and shape of a fountain can also differ dramatically: while a single, simple plume has ultimate elegance, there is rugged power in a gushing jet, and tranquillity in a bubble just

breaking the surface of a large flat pool. There are innumerable different designs of fountain, and ways in which they can be used, but as with all garden design, the simpler statements work best.

The background to a fountain should always be carefully considered. A fountain seen against a pale sky will become almost invisible; if viewed against a darker plane of hedging or planting, the plume will be thrown into sharp relief.

Uses: The prime use of a fountain is to draw the eye and form a focal point, whether this be dramatic or low-key. A secondary function, and one that can be vital in a fish pond, is to aerate the water in the pool. In addition to this, there is no doubt that a water jet has a cooling influence, both real and psychological.

Construction: The height and volume of water in a fountain will depend on the size of pump driving it. Today, virtually all pumps are submersible, safe, relatively cheap to run, and have a long life. A valve is often incorporated between the pump and the jet, and this can be used to control the volume of water reaching the head.

Different fountain heads create different effects, from a single narrow plume to a widely dispersed ring of separate jets. A jet can also be set beneath the water, when it will create a bubble or simply ripple the surface.

Pumps today are completely sealed and therefore very safe, but it should be remembered that electricity is a potential killer in a garden, particularly when it is in the proximity of water. Correct wiring, run through a conduit, is essential, as is a circuit-breaker connected into its own separate socket. If in doubt, *always* employ a qualified electrician.

Contrasting & associating materials: Fountains are essentially self-contained, and although usually set in a pool, they can issue from a boulder or other feature. They should take their cue from the design of the overall composition. I have recently designed a number of highly reflective acrylic pyramids which have bubble fountains issuing from slots in the surface, creating the most stunning effects in sunlight. Don't be shy, the possibilities are endless.

Not only are fountains effective used as focal points, but they can also serve to divide a space or pierce a vista, encouraging you to pause before moving on.

STREAMS

By placing a few simple stones across this stream the designer has succeeded in creating a bridge that doubles as a weir. This has the effect of backing the water up, allowing it to cascade over the feature as a small waterfall. This creates both movement and sound, two vital ingredients in a large-scale composition of this kind.

Characteristics: Streams are, by definition, natural features, and it is not easy to reproduce this effect. The manner in which a contrived stream flows through the garden will inevitably make it a major design element, and you will have to decide where it will start or finish, whether you need to cross it, whether you want to plant the margins, and how it will relate to the garden around it. Before you begin, go and look at examples of the real thing; sketch, take photographs, and get a feel for creation.

Streams can be short or long, narrow and rushing or wide and slow, depending on where you build them and the effect you want to achieve. They can be used within a rock garden, around outcrops from the bottom of a fall, or flowing gently through rolling lawns to enter a pool at a lower level; or, indeed, to encompass all of these.

A slope is obviously a prerequisite, and the nature of this slope will naturally affect the speed of water over the ground. A fast flow over rocks and steeply falling ground will be more dynamic and attention-seeking than a meandering affair working its way down a shallow gradient.

If you are lucky enough to possess a natural stream, it can often be modified to make it even better. Modifications could include a diversion, damming sections to form pools, weirs and falls, and creating meanders that could link in with the flowing lines of lawns and borders.

Uses: All moving water has strong directional emphasis, and will lead both feet and eye through a garden. A stream can link various parts of the composition together: it might issue from planting or a small spinney, tumble down rocks that lead to a pool, exit at the other side, flow through a boggy area, pass under a bridge, bend past a sitting area and summerhouse, and empty into a large holding pool at the bottom of the slope. It can also divide the garden, perhaps separating a controlled, formal design from a far less formal area given over to rougher grass, trees and indigenous planting.

Construction: The bed of a natural stream will be basically watertight, but if you change its direction this may not be the case. (If you tamper with a natural watercourse you may also need to let your local Water Authority know.) In this situation, the new course will need lining with a naturally impermeable material, such as clay; a job for a specialist landscape contractor.

If you are creating a new stream, avoid using concrete on its own, which tends to crack imperceptibly over a period of time, and use butyl or laminated plastic liners bedded on a cushioning layer of wet concrete. Cover the liner with more concrete, which protects the surface and allows stones to be loosely tumbled in to form a natural bed. You can spend hours painstakingly positioning rocks and stones, but forget it; nature bundles them down the banks and over the bottom in a totally random pattern, and that's the technique for you.

The size of the pool at the end of the circuit is of major importance. This will play host to a submersible pump that will draw water from the bottom pool, pump it to the top of the run, and fill the stream on the way back to the bottom. When the pump is switched on, the level of water in the lower or feeder pool will drop (more or less, according to the length of the run and the volume of water required). Unless this pool is sufficiently large, you will always need to top the water-level up because you are draining water from this pool to fill the rest of the circuit. Do this either with a hosepipe, or, in sophisticated systems, with an automatic float switch. A feeder pool with only twice the volume of the rest of the circuit will therefore lose half of its water. When you switch the pump off, the water will flow back from the stream and cause the pool to overflow, so it is worth installing an outfall pipe to prevent this from happening.

Contrasting & associating materials: Streams associate with all those materials found in a natural setting: rock, planting, grass and trees. Build bridges to fit into their surroundings, construct paving for any adjoining sitting areas from natural materials, and be sure that the design of any adjacent building is in harmony.

WATERFALLS

Characteristics: If you are lucky enough to live in an upland area, and part of your garden contains a natural stream and waterfall, you will know just how beautiful this feature is. 'Fallingwater', one of Frank Lloyd Wright's most dynamic houses, was set amid a series of falls, with water sliding and sweeping around the architecture. Few of us have the opportunity to match this, but the drama of falling water is a powerful one.

Natural falls, both real and created, have a gloriously informal character, but it is perfectly possible to create a dramatic, closely controlled formal waterfall within a supremely architectural framework. This might take the form of a classical cascade issuing from a high terrace or falling on either side of steps (both of which have considerable historical precedent), or a sharply detailed leading edge design that uses polished steel, glass and concrete to form a series of water chutes and falls. The great American contemporary landscape architect, Lawrence Halprin, designs massive and wonderful cascades in sharply modelled and board-finished concrete. These interpret the streams and falls of his beloved high sierra, but in a style that is timeless.

Unfortunately, such imitations all too often fail to live up to the real thing, and at worst are downright degrading. Scale is all important here: the usual fault is

a lack of boldness, where the feature is reduced to insignificance. Just occasionally, the pendulum swings the other way, and boldness becomes gross and overblown; there is not much to choose between the two. The commonest fault is to build a large feature and then have an underpowered pump that results in a feeble fall. If you build big, then power generously; if the fall is a small one (which is often equally, if not more, effective), then still use a generous pump. You can easily valve it down to the flow you want, but it is impossible to do the opposite.

Uses: Waterfalls are great linking elements, leading the eye down a slope, or a dramatic change of level. They can reinforce the line of a path or steps, create enormous movement, and act as major focal points. One of their great attributes is the sound of tumbling water, and large falls can even be used to combat background noise such

CONSTRUCTING A WATERFALL
A submersible pump circulates the water from the feeder pool to the top pool.

Water level

Stone to form fall

Butyl liner

Liners bonded with mastic and sandwiched between stones

Sand

Feeder pool

CREATING A NATURAL SETTING
Always build falls to look as natural as possible, bearing in mind that the lower or feeder pool should always have a considerably greater volume than the higher pool. Be sure to keep any surrounding rocks and planting in scale with the overall feature.

The Japanese influence is strong here, as demonstrated by the depth of understanding apparent in the dynamics of how the water has been used and the way in which the surrounding rocks have been set to maximum effect. The whole scene is strongly sculptural, the vertical stones serving to emphasize and enhance the line of the fall.

as that of traffic. In Halprin's Freeway Park in Seattle, the huge waterfalls completely drown out the noise of an eight-lane highway that passes underneath !

Construction: All waterfalls take skill to set and build properly. If you are thinking of tackling the job yourself, go and see how nature has done it: almost invariably, pretty well!

For a natural design, stone will need to be set at a specific angle, or bedding plane, to match any surrounding outcrops; the lip will need to be angled to shed water in the pattern you want; and ancillary rocks, such as fall stones, can be positioned under the flow to throw the water away from the face. After many years of experience, I have found that butyl liners are the best for keeping pools and falls watertight, but it is important to set the rocks and cover the pool floor in concrete; this both hides and protects the liner, and makes it easier to bed the various stones. The essential thing is to prevent water running back behind the liners, and out of the pool.

Contemporary falls often use a lip of glass, slate or marble to give a clean, crisp cascade, and these usually need a drip channel cut into the underside to prevent water running back under the sill. I am now using half-sections of black-painted guttering as a lip (in a variety of metals), set with the rounded side uppermost. The water spills off this perfectly cleanly, and it is both simple and cheap to install. Fibreglass and plastic pre-formed waterfalls are available in garden centres, but they are, on the whole, inferior, and should be avoided.

Contrasting & associating materials: These will depend entirely on the character of the feature, which will in turn reflect the character of the garden. Informal falls blend beautifully into well-built rock gardens in a relaxed part of the garden; crisp, contemporary falls look good with similar materials; and in a formal, possibly classical garden, sawn natural stone, gravel and wide lawns will complement the picture.

FORMAL SWIMMING POOLS

To an architectural designer, this composition would surely be pure heaven! There is line, form, a subtly reflective background and above all simplicity. Following the principle that form follows function, this pool not only looks stunning, but will also be a joy to swim in. The design certainly fulfills the maxim that less is more.

Characteristics: Open-air swimming pools can either be sited close to the house, where they become part of the hard landscaping that surrounds the building, or farther away, when they can be completely screened. Both are acceptable in design terms, and the choice will be influenced by the amount of use the pool gets, and the climate in which you live. Around the Mediterranean and in California, where the summers are long and the winters mild, a pool can be used for virtually the whole year, and as part of everyday life is probably best sited near the house. In more temperate climates its use is inevitably more limited, and since the sight of an empty shell, or a sheet of freezing water, can be extremely depressing on a cold winter's day, you will do better to site the pool some distance away.

The use of classical columns, balustrade and Grecian statues smack more of an excavated Roman villa than a twentieth-century garden, and almost always looks ostentatious, but most formal pools have a strong architectural link of some kind with the area around them, which should naturally include changing rooms, the pool plant, and associated hard landscaping. Indoor pools are usually built as an integral part of the house, or as an extension to it, perhaps in a nearby barn or similar outbuilding.

Formal pools, whether indoor or out, are usually rectangular (the best shape for serious swimmers), sometimes with rounded ends, and are occasionally circular. You also need to think hard and long about the finish you want for the sides and bottom of the pool. Blue mosaic tiles are without doubt the most dull and overworked finish devised by man. Use mosaic by all means, but be aware that the designs need to be really well executed, in bold shapes and patterns, to avoid a fussy result. My taste tends to be rather purist and a single strong colour is generally enough for me: what about using deep red, green, or even black? Black is gloriously elegant as it tends to conceal the depth of the pool, though it has to be said that swimming in a black pool can be pretty creepy – like courting disaster from the creature of the black lagoon! David Hockney is painting the walls of pools, and you could do the same; in fact, you can do nearly anything that appeals to you, so think about it.

As a final consideration, remember that any formal pool will be a dominant feature, and if it becomes the central focus of the overall composition, then the rest of the garden may have to radiate out from it. If this is the effect you want, then that's fine, but it may be a good reason for

This glorious riot of a composition simply hums with vibrancy and colour. Admittedly, the climate is sub-tropical or Mediterranean, which shows the strong colours to their best advantage, but it's a pity that few designers work in such a confident way. Although the pool is small it is fitted with a powerful jet, allowing you to swim against the tide.

planning it as a self-contained area, screened by planting, contouring or some form of trellising. The need for shelter may be an additional reason: in a temperate climate, protection from walls, hedges or fences may dictate an entirely separate garden in its own right.

Uses: Apart from its obvious use, a swimming pool will be a major focus of life in the garden, and will provide room for sitting, dining, entertaining, barbecuing, and a good few other things besides. An intelligent design will incorporate all these, and wrap the space in planting. Linkage is important if the pool is set away from the house, and you will need to think about pathways, pergolas and other such features.

Construction: There are a number of different ways of building a pool, but despite what the kit manufacturers say, unless you are a builder this is a skilled job best left to the professionals.

Constructional materials for below-ground pools include concrete blocks, sprayed with additional concrete; pure sprayed concrete shells with suitable reinforcing; and liners of various types that are fitted into a framework. You will also find above-ground pools, normally fabricated from liners within some kind of timber or metal frame. While these are relatively cheap and easy to erect, they often look pretty terrible and cause havoc if they are punctured!

The siting of plant and machinery, as well as changing facilities, will also have to be considered.

Contrasting & associating materials: A formal pool will sit comfortably in a formal situation. If the setting is a traditional one, then all the traditional materials such as natural stone, brick and similar surfaces will be suitable. If the composition is a contemporary one, then decking, precast paving, plastics and imitation turf can all come into play. Many people view the latter with horror, but if you look upon it as waterproof carpet, and choose colours other than green, then all will be well.

You will certainly need a large budget, not to mention a spectacular setting, for a design on this scale! This superb pool, with its hint of classicism, provides a perfect example of understatement in design. The dramatic change of level gives the impression that the water is sliding off the edge of the hill and into the landscape beyond.

INFORMAL SWIMMING POOLS

Informality in design, with its sweeping shapes and dynamic forms, often brings with it a sense of space and movement. The secret here lies in the simplicity of line and the choice of materials that blend into the surrounding landscape. There is an enormous environmental responsibility involved in dealing with a situation of this kind.

Characteristics: Here the scope is infinite, and virtually any shape can be used in an asymmetric or informal setting. Having said that, there is always a temptation to ignore the basic rules of simplicity or control: the ubiquitous kidney shape is probably the weakest and least satisfactory design shape ever conceived. Rectangles can also be used in an informal situation, and can often be mixed with curves to build up elegant shapes.

Americans, thanks in the main to their benign climate, are past masters at designing and building swimming pools. If you are thinking of building a pool, consult as many American books as you can, and notice how the finished pools are not only beautiful shapes, but are linked to their immediate and wider setting.

The hard landscape materials adjoining a free-form pool might, for example, be brushed aggregate concrete, other fluid surfaces such as industrial plastic flooring, or decking which can be cut to shape. And in order to link the pool into the wider garden and the landscape beyond, spoil

from the excavation could form the basis for subtle and gentle contours, reinforced by planting and approached by sweeping paths. These shapes could be repeated in the surrounding lawns and borders, and the whole design could take its cue from the rolling countryside beyond.

Once again, the pool floor is important – while sweeping mosaic patterns in contrasting colours can be dramatic and link with the pool shape, a single colour often works best.

Uses: Much the same as for formal pools, except that the whole composition will be rather more laid-back and relaxed.

Construction: If you are designing your own pool, the best way of creating satisfactory curves is to draw them out with a pair of compasses, sweeping one curve into the next in a naturally flowing pattern, before transferring the final design to the chosen site. Concrete sprayed over a reinforced frame is one of the most popular methods of

constructing free-form pools, as it will easily conform to any shape. As with formal pools, construction is really a job for the expert.

Contrasting & associating materials: Free-form pools call for fluid materials around them, or ones that can be easily cut to shape, such as decking. Let your imagination rip: you could create stunning effects with large boulders set within the surrounding paving, or a waterfall cascading into the deep end. The sensation of swimming under falling water is unsurpassed, and kids love it. You could have pool accessories such as gushing jets, slides, diving boards and all the rest; sculpture could be specially commissioned to pick up the shape or character of the pool. If it can also be swum through, or under, so much the better! But always try and choose everything to blend with the overall design, rather than tacking on extra detail as an afterthought. Design is about a creating a total environment, not just dislocated parts of it.

To me this has to be the ultimate swimming pool, although a degree of courage would be needed to swim in it! To produce such an effect, the change of level at the far side need not be very great, but should be just enough to break the sight line and create the sensation that you are swimming along the edges of the world.

ROCK FEATURES

Traditional rock gardens tend to be relatively labour-intensive features as they require regular attention if weeds are not to swamp the other plants. The stones used here, which have acquired a rich and handsome patina of lichen, are of an ample size, and they have been set to a bedding plane that works its way down the slope.

Characteristics: Rock gardens, rock outcrops and rock features are all members of a family that has been much abused. At their best, they mirror nature in the closer confines of the garden, and act as wonderful hosts for a wide selection of specialist planting. At worst, the currant bun rockery is a travesty of the real thing, often built from discarded lumps of concrete, and with more weeds than intended planting.

A true rockery will draw its inspiration from an upland landscape where rock outcrops naturally, and this is where you should go to get a feel of how to choose and set rock properly.

Different rocks have different characteristics: some are smooth, some deeply fissured, some split down their grain, while colours range from the speckled granites to dark red sandstones and pale limestones. The prime rule is to try and use a local stone, which is in plentiful supply. Fine stone found only in one region, which is probably also in limited supply, will never look completely at home anywhere else, and the cost of transporting it may well be exorbitant.

As an alternative to natural stone, there are a number of excellent imitation stones available. These are made from resins, fibreglass, and crushed stone, and at their best they can be indistinguishable from the real thing.

Uses: Rock gardens, outcrops or just large boulders are focal points of differing intensity, but all provide vertical emphasis which demands attention. They can be used either as a vehicle for planting alpines and other specialist material, or left unplanted, as an outcrop in a grassed area, in woodland, or even in a paved area where one or more large boulders can double as seats. A raised area such as this can also act as a screen or pivot, concealing another part of the garden and providing a feeling of mystery as a path winds into the space to reveal a secondary view.

Construction: The secret of using rock effectively lies in understanding how it outcrops naturally. When you see it in the landscape, all you will see is the top surface; the rest, like an iceberg, is concealed beneath the ground. This immediately presents a problem, for since the material is relatively expensive you will want to get visual value for your money, yet if you simply perch rocks on the surface the result will always look artificial. This may be valid as sculpture, but it will never look natural.

You will also see that rock in the landscape outcrops in lines, following the strata below the surface, and at a set angle known as the bedding plane. A rock garden should also be set out in this way. Start by choosing a single stone, and set this in position to give you the line and the angle for the rest of the rocks. This keystone should, like all the other stones, be sunk into the ground to at least half its depth. One or two outlying rocks can be used to link the feature into the wider garden, and these, too, should follow the imaginary line of strata to give an impression of an extensive network beneath the garden.

The vast majority of alpine plants enjoy a gritty, free-draining soil, and it is important never to use subsoil when building a rock garden. Scree (fragments of rock broken down by natural weathering) can be used to form a top surface that will provide excellent drainage, and through which plants can grow. Rock gardens often look at their best in an informal part of the garden, but natural-looking outcrops can add high drama around a house or swimming pool.

Contrasting & associating materials: Rock looks its best alongside other natural materials from the same family. It would be a mistake to mix slate rockery stone with Cotswold or golden stone walling and York or grey stone paving; but in the west of England you will see slate paving, walling and rock looking superb together, with each element playing its individual role.

The Japanese have an innate understanding of rock and how it can be positioned to greatest effect in the garden. Using rock in such arrangements underlines the affinity of Japanese gardens with the wider landscape. In this highly stylized composition, the clipped shrub echoes and enhances the shape of the stone.

CONSTRUCTING A ROCK FEATURE
Set the rocks carefully at a similar angle or bedding plane to simulate a natural outcrop.

SUMMERHOUSES

This delightful display is the epitome of a traditional English country garden, with its sprawling roses, fragrant honeysuckle and the most inviting of garden buildings tucked away behind the abundant flowers.

Small buildings with shady interiors are always irresistibly enticing, all the more so when they are tempered with planting and set below such an elegant roof.

Characteristics: It has come to pass that any old garden building, from a shed to a chalet, is now called a summerhouse – particularly by manufacturers keen to hype their products.

Traditionally, a summerhouse was just that: a small building, built from local materials in a wide range of vernacular styles, usually set at some distance from the main house, to provide a hub for summer sitting, eating, entertaining and, first and foremost, the grand old habit of afternoon tea in the garden. Typically a product of a temperate climate, a summerhouse was designed to provide shelter from showers and wind, as well as from hot summer sun. Some houses can be turned round on a pivot to chase the sun, but this can position it at odds with sight lines and the rest of the garden alignment.

Uses: As a major focal point and a centre of summer inactivity. Afternoon tea may have diminished in importance, but as a sitting place, surrounded by a terrace, the summerhouse can play an important role in the overall garden design. It does, however, suggest that you have time to sit and relax. If you do, then this is the building for you. The temptation will be to use a summerhouse as a storeroom for general garden junk. Don't! If you need a shed, get one.

Construction: Stone, brick and timber are all suitable construction materials, with timber being the cheapest and most easily worked, and therefore the commonest. Construction techniques will be the same as for any small building; your summerhouse will require sound foundations, flooring, walls and a roof. Some buildings are available in kit form, but these are often visually and physically flimsy.

Contrasting & associated materials: Materials used for the summerhouse should blend with those used for the house or surroundings, though timber will feel comfortable in most settings. The same link can be made with adjoining paving.

128

GAZEBOS

This really is a room with a view, which is what gazebos are all about. Both the airy structure and the simple furniture are perfectly in harmony, and I particularly like the characterful climber trained over the roof.

Characteristics: These are, correctly, garden buildings that are specifically set to embrace a view. In reality, the name has been taken by manufacturers, and many gardeners, to mean anything from a shed to a summerhouse, however crude, which can be plonked down virtually anywhere.

Gazebos come in many different styles. They were originally landscape features, when good views were more prevalent, and would, and still should, reflect the style and the mood of the composition around them. They can be modern or traditional, small or large, but in the final analysis the view is the most important thing.

Uses: While some gazebos are set on top of a hill or at the end of a vista, I feel that they are at their most effective when tucked away with a degree of secrecy that makes them essentially informal and all the more attractive. Such places are to be happened upon, rather than seeking visual attention.

Construction: Like other garden buildings, they will be constructed from the widest range of materials: brick, stone, timber, metal, or a mixture of any of these. Very few are available for sale; the best will be built by craftsmen on site.

Contrasting & associating materials: Gazebos should be low key, likewise the surroundings. Informality is the key here. Floors can be old paving, brick, chipped bark, or simply beaten soil. Planting is a perfect foil, to blend the structure into its surroundings.

The style of some gazebos can be highly stylized, and while this is permissible, the siting of such a feature has to be undertaken with care to prevent it from clashing with the surrounding garden. The gravel path here echoes the white columns of the building.

SHEDS

Well-constructed plain wooden sheds have a certain no-nonsense elegance. Once it has weathered, a timber structure will blend into virtually any setting; this shed is softened by the random planting which surrounds it and the grand tree growing behind.

This beautifully built stone shed will last almost indefinitely; it is solid enough to act as a house, and many would welcome it as such! The plaque set over the door makes an attractive extra detail.

Characteristics: Every garden needs at least one shed. Sheds are the utility workhorses of the wider composition and can serve a multitude of purposes. They are by their nature usually mundane structures, and it makes sense to screen them or tuck them away in an unobtrusive position. Access by a sound, wide path is important, as is some kind of adjoining hardstanding on which to park wheelbarrows and tools, or for use as an outdoor work space.

Most can be bought prefabricated, and as a general rule it is worth going for the best quality shed you can afford; it will pay dividends in length of service. It is also worth buying a size larger than you think you will need; sheds will always fill up faster than you expect. Styles vary enormously, and are available with double- or single-pitched roofs, and with doors and windows in different positions. Lean-to sheds that fit neatly against an existing wall can also be useful .

Uses: For storing tools, equipment, furniture, and anything else you can think of. Ideal as a workshop, for housing specialist equipment such as a filtration plant for a swimming pool, or, suitably modified, for animals of various kinds.

Construction: Although usually bought in kit form, and assembled on site, it is quite possible to build your own shed. Straightforward carpentry skills are needed, and the great advantage is that you can create the size and style you want. The shed will need a sound foundation: a concrete slab cast over a consolidated hardcore base is ideal, and paving slabs bedded in mortar over a similar base are also acceptable, though often unnecessarily expensive.

Woodwork will need regular applications of non-toxic preservative, and bought sheds will usually have been treated prior to sale. Depending on the size of building, the roof will shed considerable amounts of rainwater. A water butt to collect this water is always a good idea.

Contrasting & associating materials: Sheds should be simply sited and suitably screened with trellis, hedging, fencing, walling, or a combination of any of these. Close to a house, a shed and utility area could be designed to form an extension of the architecture. Next to a path, a shed can play host to overhead beams, covered with climbers, that will both soften its outline and blend it into the wider garden.

GREENHOUSES

Characteristics: Glass-sided and glass-roofed buildings providing a warm environment, protection for tender plants in winter, and suitable conditions for propagation, growing on, and a multitude of other horticultural activities. Traditionally set in the vegetable garden, many greenhouses are attractive enough to become focal points in their own right, and merit a more prominent position in the composition. Careful siting is crucial – as with any small building there is a tendency to plonk greenhouses down anywhere, which can spell disaster in a well-conceived design.

Greenhouses are normally rectangular, but there are other shapes and styles available; hexagonal and circular houses will create interesting design possibilities for the areas around them, and lean-to greenhouses can fit neatly against a wall. Like sheds, greenhouses need good paths for access, and ample hardstanding around them. For a heated greenhouse, electric power lines from the nearest source will need to be buried safely in a conduit. Paraffin heaters provide a cheaper form of heating, but they require regular maintenance and can be hazardous if knocked over.

Uses: All the above, but also for growing specialist plants such as cacti, alpines, vines, orchids, as well as tomatoes, herbs in winter, pot flowers for the house, and tender or unusual species.

Construction: Greenhouses are usually constructed from either timber or metal alloy. While the first often look better and more substantial, owing to the thicker sizing of the framework, the latter usually last a good deal longer. Timber houses can be built from either hardwood or softwood (cedar is popular), but all will need regular treatment with non-toxic preservative. Both types of house must be positioned on an absolutely horizontal base, to prevent the frame from twisting, and subsequent difficulty in fitting the glass. This base usually consists of a number of courses of brickwork, on to which the frame is bolted.

Contrasting & associating materials: Gravel can form an excellent surround, as can brushed aggregate concrete. Greenhouses can be planned as focal points in either the vegetable garden or the decorative garden, with the composition radiating out from them.

The greenhouse is almost incidental in this profusion of planting. This makes sense as metal greenhouses can look rather austere in many settings, requiring the softening influence either of plants or some kind of screening.

Using a greenhouse to grow plants that would not survive in the open garden can be enormously satisfying. The chance to build up a collection of well-ordered pots and containers only adds to the pleasure.

TREEHOUSES

There is a justifiable element of trickery here as both the treehouse and the enormous supporting branches of the tree below it are held up with substantial metal poles set in concrete. The overall results are superb.

Characteristics: The best treehouses are for grown-ups – I once had dinner in a fully blown dining-room 12m (40ft) up in the branches of a huge chestnut tree. Built by a professional carpenter, it was large enough to hold a dozen people and had a built-in sink, dishwasher and fridge. It was interesting to be up there in a high wind! The steps up to it were terrifying; the way down less so, particularly after a good meal and a few glasses of claret.

More typical, less sophisticated affairs are ideal for kids. These should always be sturdily built, with safety in mind, in a large tree that is absolutely sound. The most basic treehouse is simply a stout platform, reached either by climbing the tree itself, or via a rope ladder. A more elaborate one may have walls and a roof, with an adjoining staircase.

Uses: For all kinds of play; for the grown-ups, all kinds of activities.

Construction: Invariably of timber, treehouses should be adequately sized and securely fixed. There is always an element of risk in such a situation, so the sounder the construction and the safer the access, the better it will be for everyone. Don't build a treehouse unless you have a substantial tree – there will inevitably be some damage, with a few boughs cut back and nails driven in. Most people will be able to tackle such a project, and it can be ideal for kids, with the correct supervision.

Contrasting & associating materials: The most spectacular treehouses can become focal points; more often, they will blend comfortably into an orchard or spinney.

PLAYHOUSES

The local gang hanging out at their favourite joint, and enjoying it too! Solid logs make an excellent material for building playhouses and, if they are well constructed, such buildings should last a lifetime.

Characteristics: At their best, these are magical places, often made by children themselves or an enlightened grown-up. While safety must always be a consideration, the best playhouses are often ramshackle affairs, built from materials to hand, and readily demolished on a whim or in a high wind. Children naturally like to hide away, and the fact that the playhouses are usually hidden from view is probably just as well, for they are no architectural masterpieces. The argument that such structures should be in full view of the kitchen window is nonsense, certainly as far as the children are concerned.

At their worst, playhouses come in the form of horrible plastic Wendy houses, and are filled with ready-made toys that leave not an ounce of imagination to the child. The simplest approach, which can be the best, is just to cast a sheet over a clothes-line, climbing frame or other piece of play equipment. Such tents can be quickly modified, and are retrievable in case of rain.

Uses: Imaginative play.

Construction: Timber is the favourite material, with, if home-made, the addition of anything else that comes to hand. Ideally, playhouses should be sound, but with the potential for expansion. Purpose-built houses, like purpose-built gardens, tend to appeal less to the child; they are less flexible, last indefinitely, and end up as follies in later life.

Contrasting & associating materials: The best playhouses are hidden away, and so do not associate with anything much. Probably the best way.

PLAY EQUIPMENT

Characteristics: Although you can move some of the lighter play equipment around, major elements will, to all intents and purposes, be fixed in one position for a considerable length of time.

The choice is wide: swings, slides, climbing frames, see-saws, sandpits or sandboxes, and so on. Many of these can be bought ready-made, but prices and sturdiness will vary enormously, and as a general rule, you get what you pay for. Bent metal equipment, although relatively cheap, is neither attractive nor particularly long-lasting, especially if there are several boisterous children using it. There is, on the other hand, an increasing amount of really excellent timber equipment coming on to the market, including wonderful forts and other buildings. These look handsome and really do stand up to an enormous amount of wear, and some have slides and climbing frames built into them. Most of these units are modular, so you can extend the play area over a period of time.

As a general rule, try and group equipment in one area. This will contain the inevitably busy outline of the pieces and allow a watchful eye to be concentrated in one place.

Don't forget, either, the obvious potential of features already in the garden. A strong branch is an obvious candidate for a swing, while stout lengths of logs can be arranged and fixed in various patterns to create fascinating climbing structures; large-diameter logs can be set upright in the ground to form aerial stepping stones; ropes slung from tree to tree can be great for climbing across or used for swinging across a stream;

sand play areas of all shapes and sizes can be easily introduced. In other words, always bear safety in mind but use your imagination; the results will be great fun for all concerned.

Uses: Play!

Construction: It is particularly important to fix bought equipment firmly, as it is often light and can tip over easily. Always follow the manufacturer's instructions, and if necessary err on the side of caution where jobs like setting legs in concrete are concerned. Timber equipment should also be firmly fixed, usually in concrete foundations. Remember, the more comprehensive the equipment, the more children will come and play on it, and the more safety-conscious you need to be.

Much of the equipment can, however, be made at home, and timber again will be the obvious choice. Hardwoods are usually more durable than soft, and generously sized, sturdy timbers are essential. Beware splinters on any wood, particularly on rougher surfaces such as railway sleepers. Always finish things off as smoothly as possible with sandpaper. Non-toxic preservative should be applied to all wooden equipment at regular intervals. Straightforward carpentry skills are all that is required, and these are projects in which the kids will be delighted to become involved!

You need also to think about the ground underneath the play equipment. Grass is soft but wears out quickly; perhaps the best surface is a thick layer of chipped bark

I wish I'd had such a cleverly constructed play area when I was a child! This is an excellent example of a well-thought-out, well-integrated and sturdy design that not only looks good, but also works well and is bound to get plenty of use.

contained within a framework of boards. This is both easy on the knees and looks unobtrusive.

Contrasting & associating materials: Play areas tend to look best in the more informal parts of the garden, where there is more likely to be ample room to run around and generally make chaos. A background of planting and a surround of lawn is all that is needed. A shed or somewhere else to store toys, bikes and all the rest, is invaluable.

RAISED BEDS

introduce a specific soil type that might not be present in the wider garden, allowing you to grow ericaceous or other specialist plants.

The curve of this raised bed is echoed by the circular paving pattern of granite setts that adjoins it. The bed is constructed from stout logs set into the ground at slightly varying heights, with planting encouraged to grow over the edge to soften the line. Similar logs, specifically for this purpose and pre-treated against rot, are widely available.

Characteristics: Raised beds can be both practical and attractive in virtually any garden. They bring planting up to an easy working height, which can be particularly useful for people who are handicapped. Raising plants closer to eye level makes them look more mature and means that small species such as alpines can also be enjoyed more easily. Most beds will be rectangular in outline, blending naturally with terraced and architectural areas close to the house, as well as with steps and changes in level.

Materials will include most of those used for boundaries, and will take their cue from the surrounding garden and locality. Timber can also be used on its own, in the form of heavy baulks such as railway sleepers, or, where load-bearing is a consideration (as on a roof garden), by using boards for the sides of beds. Sleepers are particularly useful and, because of their weight,

can be bedded on a foundation of well-compacted soil, making sure they are absolutely level. They are best laid horizontally in courses, or cut down to about half their length and set vertically close together in the ground. This vertical treatment is highly suitable for logs, and paving slabs, too, can be set upright and bedded securely in concrete. However, they tend to look very hard, and need plenty of softening with prostrate plants to flop down over the edges.

Uses: Raised beds provide a useful growing space for a wide range of plants, including shrubs, herbaceous perennials, alpines, annuals, bulbs and, not least, vegetables and herbs. They are ideal for places where it is impossible to plant directly into the ground, such as a completely paved courtyard, balcony, or roof garden. An added advantage is that it becomes possible to

Construction: Walling materials such as brick or stone will need foundations that are twice the width of the walls. Good drainage is essential if the bed is not to become waterlogged, and as the walls are built, pipes should be inserted just above the surrounding ground level, spaced 900mm (3ft) apart, to drain away excess water. If the bed is based on earth, the ground should first be forked over, and a 150mm (6in) layer of hardcore or broken stone laid on top. A layer of turf should then be placed upside down over the hardcore, and at least 450mm (18in) of clean topsoil for the planting. This may need topping up after six months or so, to compensate for settling. If the bed is built on a hard surface, a 150mm (6in) layer of hardcore or crushed stone should be placed on the bottom and the soil built up as above.

Railway sleepers can be laid in a staggered bond like bricks, and for additional stability should be drilled to accept steel reinforcing rods which can be driven well into the ground. Raised beds constructed with board sides will need a protective lining of some kind. At its simplest, this will be black plastic sheeting stapled to the inside, but for a longer life, fibreglass boxes, with drainage holes in the bottom can be made up to fit individual beds.

Raised beds make a useful feature on a roof garden. These should be filled with a lightweight soil mix placed over a sheet of geo-textile and a drainage layer of clay granules.

Contrasting & associating materials: This will once again depend on the immediate garden surroundings. Brick or stone beds may echo similar materials elsewhere, while the darker colour of railway sleepers will set up a dramatic contrast with pale gravels and pale precast concrete slabs. Boards can be painted or stained to pick up a surrounding colour scheme, and will link naturally with timber decking.

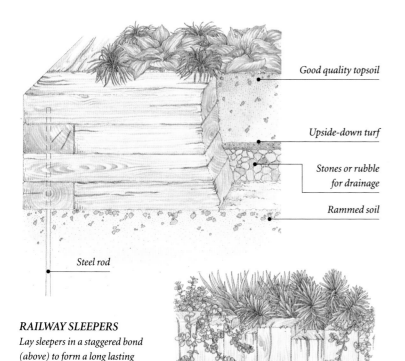

Good quality topsoil

Upside-down turf

Stones or rubble
for drainage

Rammed soil

Steel rod

In this strongly linear pattern, the raised beds and paving naturally lead the eye down to the informal seating area beneath the tree at the far end. Both pergola and planting are superbly generous, forming a magical tunnel.

RAILWAY SLEEPERS

Lay sleepers in a staggered bond (above) to form a long lasting raised bed. Thread reinforcing rods through holes and drive them into the ground to ensure stability. Alternatively, set sections of sleepers vertically at different heights (right) to form a rhythmical design.

Sleepers haunched in
concrete or rammed soil

SLAB PLANTER

Use paving slabs positioned side by side and firmly set in concrete for a low-cost planter.

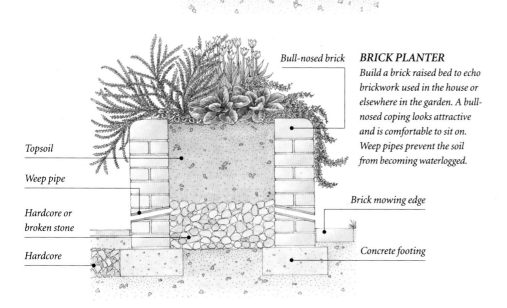

Bull-nosed brick

BRICK PLANTER

Build a brick raised bed to echo brickwork used in the house or elsewhere in the garden. A bull-nosed coping looks attractive and is comfortable to sit on. Weep pipes prevent the soil from becoming waterlogged.

Topsoil

Weep pipe

Hardcore or
broken stone

Hardcore

Brick mowing edge

Concrete footing

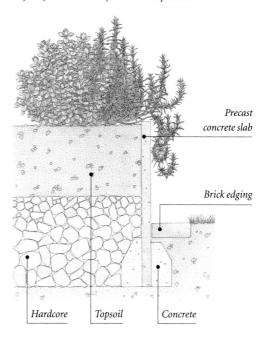

Precast
concrete slab

Brick edging

Hardcore   Topsoil   Concrete

BUILT-IN SEATING

This is an excellent example of a dual-purpose feature in which the seat doubles up as a retaining wall holding back the higher ground to the left. Such a feature provides a powerful design element, the curve of the seat subtly leading the eye towards the grass path and the area beyond with a further echo in the adjoining paving.

Characteristics: Built-in seating can be used in many situations, as a space-saving feature that can be incorporated into a totally designed outside living environment. Seats can be built into the right angle formed by two walls or raised beds, constructed as an extension to a barbecue or water feature, or designed as an integral part of a flight of steps.

Timber is often used for construction, and this is easily worked to virtually any pattern or shape, and can even be designed with a hinged top to provide storage space within. Materials are often combined: a brick or stone base, for example, can be run out from an adjoining feature or wall of the same material, and given a timber top. It could also be topped with precast concrete slabs or other type of paving.

In the wider garden, seats built around trees can be used to provide good focal points. Many ready-made designs are unnecessarily fussy, with multi-faceted sides; it is perfectly possible to build seats to your own design in simple square or rectangular shapes, making them big enough to double up as seat, table, lounger and play surface. You will occasionally see delightful metal seats, made from shaped steel or iron similar to that used in park fences; these are still available but expensive. If you inherit one, it will be well worth repairing.

Uses: As seats, obviously, but also as focal points, loungers, and play surfaces.

Construction: There is a wide choice of suitable materials, with timber being the most commonly used. A brick or stone base must be built off suitable foundations. Where a seat is worked into a flight of steps, it can be incorporated to one side, to run into surrounding planting, or the edge of a lawn, pool or other feature. The seat will be an extension of a tread, 30–45cm (12–18in) high, and could be fronted with paving of some kind to echo that used close by. A seat round a tree should be generous in its proportions, perhaps 2.5m (8ft) or even 3m (10ft) square. All timber seating can be constructed using straightforward carpentry skills, whereas metal seats will need to be made by a craftsman blacksmith.

Contrasting & associating materials: Seats are usually built as an extension of the features that they adjoin, being built from the same materials. This should provide a natural harmony in either a traditional or a more contemporary situation.

WOODEN SEATING AROUND A TREE

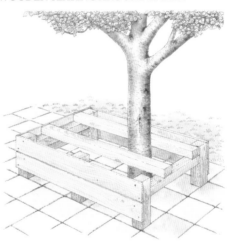

A large seat will allow for a range of activities, but keep the basic framework in proportion to the tree it surrounds.

Nail or screw slats on top of the framework, being careful to leave adequate growing space around the tree trunk.

BARBECUES

What charisma! Here is the ultimate example of one-upmanship in barbecuing. The barbecue itself appears to have been constructed in a thoroughly practical way from part of an old chimney.

Characteristics: You either are, or are not a barbecue fanatic, but should you be one of those who cannot resist the attraction of alfresco eating, then a built-in barbecue may be just the thing for you. The advantage over a portable model is sheer size; you can build something to feed half the neighbourhood, if necessary, instead of cooking in endless rotation and never getting a meal yourself! It also allows you to design the barbecue either as an island feature, allowing circulation around it, or against a wall or other feature; and to provide for ample work tops and storage space, along with integrated seating.

A barbecue can provide a focus for an outside living and entertaining area, becoming part of a carefully considered composition of built-in seating, raised beds, overhead beams and planting, the latter including herbs to flavour the cooking.

The siting of a barbecue needs to be thought about carefully, in relation to prevailing winds, afternoon and evening sun, and the proximity to

your kitchen. Don't forget your neighbours either; there is nothing more annoying than smoke pouring over the fence into your garden.

Uses: In summer, barbecues are purely for cooking, although built-in storage can be useful for all kinds of things! In winter, the cooking grids can be removed and the various split level areas will make excellent platforms for pots, which will always brighten a hard-landscaped area.

Construction: Materials for construction need to be durable, so brick and stone are both common and practical choices, while reconstituted stone, rendered and *in situ* concrete can also be used. Grids for cooking, and charcoal trays, can either be bought in kit form, or fabricated by a blacksmith or welder. Stainless steel is more expensive than other materials, but it is also the most durable and the easiest to keep clean.

Foundations for walls need to be soundly constructed, while timberwork for store doors or adjoining seats will require basic carpentry skills. Charcoal is the most commonly used fuel, but you can build space for bottled or natural gas, or electric units, into a purpose-designed housing. For the last two, this will also mean laying feeder pipes or cables (to a suitable safety standard), usually below surrounding paving. Advanced barbecues, for serious chefs, may also have chimneys, incorporating dampers and various other devices for controlling the draught.

Contrasting & associating materials: The design of the barbecue, as well as the materials used for construction, should be consistent with those found in the surrounding garden.

CONSTRUCTING A BUILT-IN BARBECUE
Brick is by far the most adaptable and practical material for building a barbecue and this design incorporates both storage and an adjoining seat.

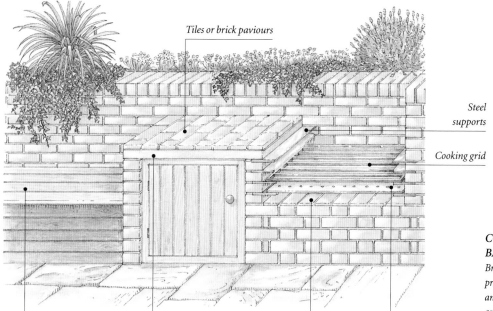

Tiles or brick paviours

Steel supports

Cooking grid

Timber seating

Concrete lintel

Paviours

Charcoal tray

ORNAMENTS, FURNITURE & SPECIAL EFFECTS

Although all these pots are of different shapes, sizes and colours, they are linked by the fact that they are all made of clay. Small pots are shown off to great effect when they are grouped together, especially if, as here, they are displayed on racks. The dark slatted fence behind sets off the bright colours of both flowers and foliage to their best advantage.

The furnishing of a garden is an ongoing process, starting on the drawing-board, where space is allocated for features, ornaments or statues in specific positions, and continuing as the garden develops. It is this furnishing that really brings the place to life, and since it is personality that determines the choice of any kind of ornamentation (you can tell much about a person by the way in which they furnish their living space, both inside and outside the house) and because of this, I rarely choose such items for my customers. I may well suggest themes and sources of supply, but at the end of the day it really is this kind of individuality that sets one garden apart from another.

Cost is, of course, another factor, and like furnishing inside the home, this can vary enormously. As with most things in the garden, you get what you pay for, but don't get carried away by the latest craze in an up-market store; you can probably buy the same thing, or something rather better, at half the price elsewhere.

Of course there are dangers in plenty: the random binge at a garden centre; the forays to antique dealers; or seduction at flower shows! We have all bought things at places like these, and lived to regret it. I own a set of wind chimes that I and hundreds of others were clamouring to buy at a particular show. They quickly drove me and the neighbours mad, came down rapidly, and have never been used again – much to the relief of all concerned. There is a lesson here!

Some homes and gardens are full of every conceivable ornament; some are sparse but stunningly elegant; many fall between these two extremes. As with most design matters, it is best to keep things simple and resist the urge to impulse buy, unless you find something that is just right for a certain situation.

I have talked a lot in this book about creating 'rooms' within the overall composition, each with a different pattern or theme that will, in turn, be reinforced by the ornamentation and furnishings chosen for them. A contemporary garden will readily accept clean, modern pieces, whether these be pots, urns, furniture or special effects. In a classical or formal composition the character of the garden will suggest a far more traditional approach. Added to this is a sensitive use of materials; stone may look good with terracotta or a traditional lead sink, but would sit rather uncomfortably with hi-tech plastic or fibreglass. In other words, it is important to think about the relationship of materials as well as the relationship of shapes. Remember, too, that pots, like plants, look better in odd-numbered groupings than in even ones: three, five, seven and nine look better than two, four, six and eight.

The problem with many gardens, and homes for that matter, is the reluctance of many people to move anything (plant or object) once it has been positioned. Apart from the physical effort involved, I'm never sure why this should be so. A room that is rearranged from time to time takes on a completely new and fresh persona, so don't get bogged down and take your garden for granted; shake it up once in a while, and you, and everyone else, will be stimulated by the outcome.

Of course, the real difference between inside and out is that a garden is alive and growing, and this means that the outline and pattern are ever changing, sometimes quite rapidly. These changes may create opportunities and niches for all kinds of ornaments: within borders, or in the angles or backdrop formed by runs of hedging; or, by altering the mowing pattern, creating settings within different heights and patterns of grass.

Hard landscape, although static, is no less versatile. Formal terraces demand regularly placed pieces whereas asymmetric designs require counterbalanced compositions. Steps are wonderful vehicles for pots, containers, statues, and all kinds of ornaments, while walls offer a vertical face for mosaics, murals, mirrors, special effects and hanging containers.

It is a sorry fact that a great deal of garden furniture is designed to look good rather than be comfortable. Comfort, at least in my book, has to come first, followed closely by a style that will fit in with the rest of the design. Many of the best features or ornaments are simply 'found objects': an old and twisted sun-bleached log, smothered with a clematis; the smooth dome of a water-worn boulder, set as a focal point at the turn of a path, or acting as an occasional seat within the paving of a terrace.

I'm not a hoarder myself, but I most certainly collect odd objects with a view to putting them 'somewhere', and although it often takes a while to find the right place, I usually get there eventually. I now have an old coal scuttle planted with a wonderful alpine sedum, an ancient cast iron boiler that plays host to a favourite hosta, a fine oak beam from our house restoration that has become a casual seat among planting, and a

couple of chimney pots that are full of trailing nasturtiums during the summer. None of these was expensive, but all are highly personal and look perfect in their final resting place. The real point is that, free or not, they give pleasure, which, at the end of the day, is what ornamentation is all about.

Illusions, although usually pretty obvious, have their purpose. Murals, mirrors and *trompe l'œil* can all create atmosphere and a feeling of space, and the visual trickery of *trompe l'œil* can also, if done with style, be used to create humour. All, by their nature, allow unlimited imagination. Children have imagination in abundance, so get them involved in the whole process; you could be surprised by the results!

This composition has a wonderfully inviting air. Benches designed with a broad back are far more comfortable to sit on than those with flimsier supports, and the curved design relates better to its softly planted surroundings than it would to one with more rigid lines.

STATUARY

Good statuary, as with much hard landscaping, can often be enhanced by a frame or the softening influence of planting. While there is humour here, there is also a fair degree of *manipulation, or perhaps good luck! Regular pruning, or slight adjustments to the position of the statue, will be required to keep this composition under control.*

While this could be used as a topiary frame, it is also valid when used as a statue in its own right. The best setting for such a piece will almost certainly be an informal one, *to mimic the natural habitat of the animal, and while the immediate surroundings are of prime importance, lighting could also be used to dramatic effect.*

Characteristics: Statues have been with us for a very long time, and were just as much at home in classic Roman outdoor rooms as they are in a contemporary garden. But beauty is in the eye of the beholder, and while the most perfectly modelled bust will appeal to some, an anguished arrangement of sculpted steel may turn others on. Of course the style and situation of the garden should influence the choice, but remember that a formal layout can be traditional or modern, and will ask for statues that are chosen accordingly.

Although figures are a common choice, statues can mimic virtually anything: animals, fish, birds and even garden gnomes, so popular in England. The last should not be written off, however much they are condemned by horticultural snobs; a sense of humour is one of the most important elements in any garden, so to hell with what the establishment says!

Uses: Statues will be greater or lesser focal points, drawing the eye to a particular part of the garden. Their placing will therefore need careful thought, and this will often have been worked out on the

drawing-board at the design stage. Statues demand attention in their own right but can also be used to give emphasis to another feature: surrounding or providing the central feature of a pool; standing in niches along the face of a wall or hedge; or flanking a doorway.

Construction: Most sculpture will be carved or cast by specialists (though this is an area where even children can create an object of worth), and materials can include natural or reconstituted stone, concrete, timber, metal and synthetics such as plastic or fibreglass, or even osier. Most will be static, but some will be plumbed for water spouts, or powered as moving features.

Contrasting & associating materials: This will be entirely dependent on the setting, though a fabulous bronze or subtle wood carving may look equally at home with both natural and man-made surfaces. Perhaps more than with anything else in the garden, this is a question of what looks and feels right. In short, it will test your eye as a creative and sensitive person.

Standing stones possess enormous power and drama. Their individual nature means that while some will look perfect in a natural setting, others can suit hi-tech surroundings.

WALL PLAQUES

OBELISKS

Characteristics: One of the most dramatic focal points of all, shaped like an upside-down exclamation mark and designed to draw the eye. The classic obelisk usually takes the form of a tapered stone needle, standing on top of four balls, which are in turn positioned on a rectangular stone base. The largest are built as monuments, and are only successful in parkland, but there are many different variations in size and form, and you should be able to find an obelisk that will suit even the smallest garden.

Uses: Positioned singly as a focal point at the end of a vista, walk or pergola. Pairs can be set to flank gates or doorways, or a number can be positioned on either side of a pathway in much the same way as topiary shapes, when they will have the effect of accelerating the view towards its end.

Construction: Obelisks are usually constructed from natural or reconstituted stone, but the shape can be elegantly created using virtually any hard material as well as by clipped and training hedging plants such as yews. Obelisks can also be constructed from specially designed trellis structures, the base taking the form of a square tub into which climbers can be planted.

Contrasting & associating materials: Obelisks are adaptable features, and while they will fit naturally into a traditional or formal garden, the larger examples can also look at home in the most informal parkland setting. Because of their simple geometry they can also be highly effective in a contemporary design, especially where they are associated with traditional materials such as natural stone, brick, and gravel, although they will also look good positioned next to high-quality precast concrete paving.

The choice of any kind of ornament is a highly individual matter, and objects often carry with them a whole collection of personal associations or even religious overtones. Great care and attention should always be taken when siting an ornamental feature; this marble plaque stands out in sharp contrast to the brick wall around it.

Characteristics: These appear in an enormous range of styles, patterns, sizes and shapes, from huge carvings in relief, set into the walls of an historic garden, to a child's school project that will give no less pleasure to the viewer. They are found all over the world, and often have a strong ethnic character. Although wall plaques tend to be popular subjects for bringing back home from holiday, it's worth remembering that what looks spectacular in one situation may look uncomfortable in another.

Uses: Like statues, plaques provide a focal point, but usually at a higher level. Being mounted on the face of a wall they naturally bring interest to the vertical plane, and can be used either singly or as a group to set up a particular pattern. They can also be fitted with a spout, allowing water to fall into a pool or bowl below.

Construction: Plaques can be made from a wide range of materials that include stone, reconstituted stone, wood, synthetics, ceramics, metal and glass. The most complicated are craftsman-made, but simpler ceramics or carvings can be more easily constructed. Where water is used, they can be plumbed to a submersible pump in the pool or bowl below.

Contrasting & associating materials: There is a suitable plaque for every conceivable situation and associating material, so choose carefully.

Although obelisks are often used singly, this little tribe is rather fun and highly individualistic. With any kind of ornamentation, positioning is all important, and these look just right nestling into the edge of the informal planting. The construction used here is unusual, and was almost certainly carried out using materials to hand.

URNS

The beauty of a well-chosen and carefully positioned urn is that it will look good throughout the year, even in the depths of winter. This stone urn has been set alongside a whole family of compatible features, including a clipped box, ivy-clad columns and trompe l'œil *trellis.*

Is this contemporary urn broken or not? Either way it provides an attractive focal point and is undoubtedly a highly personal, possibly home-made, piece. Such ornaments are full of a character and charm that is unique to their owners.

Characteristics: Most urns are classical in design, and are available in a vast range of patterns and sizes. Depending on size, they are more or less suitable for planting, but often look their best when left empty. They usually stand on a base or pedestal.

Uses: Urns are often used as focal points in a formal setting, and can be positioned singly, in pairs, groups, or flanking a door, arch, path or pergola. If they are to be planted, the larger the bowl the better, to allow for adequate root development and less frequent watering.

Construction: Lead was traditional, albeit expensive, and is still used today, but usually now of stone or reconstituted stone. Cast iron was formerly a popular material.

Fibreglass and plastic have their uses, but are simply degrading when they are used to imitate another material. Concrete urns usually look cheap, although recently there have been a number of new processes that produce a more realistic surface texture that is far more acceptable.

Contrasting & associating materials: Classical urns generally sit comfortably with most other traditional materials such as natural paving, brick, gravel, and good quality precast concrete slabs. Soft landscaping, in the form of planting, lawns and background hedges, will also create a worthwhile setting.

FOUND OBJECTS

This collection of individually collected objects is enormous fun, and will certainly be unique. Always endeavour to create a garden that reflects your own personal taste, rather than slavishly following the dictates of horticultural snobs.

Characteristics: These can be fun and inexpensive, and are things that will reflect your personality and sense of humour. They will also in all probability be unique. The term covers a miscellaneous range of items, from a gnarled old log, a coal scuttle, or rugged boulder, to a set of beautifully reflective glass balls that were originally used as floats for commercial fishing nets. They will in short be anything that catches your eye and can be used as a point of interest, somewhere in the garden.

Uses: As a major or incidental focal point, which must always be positioned with care, even if appearing not to be. Depending on the object, use might be decorative, or more practical: a log or boulder doubling as a seat, a hollowed out stone as a birdbath, a coal scuttle as a planter or a bathtub as a herb garden.

Construction: The real point is that these objects are found and subsequently used without any interference by you.

Contrasting & associating materials: Depending on the feature, the choices are legion. An old log can sit as comfortably in woodland as on a crisp concrete terrace. Use your imagination and sensitivity.

The power and movement in this superbly gnarled old log is supreme and introduces a completely different theme to the well planted terrace. It serves several purposes, as a seat, a children's climbing frame, and ultimately as a fine piece of sculpture. The only problem here will have been the difficulty of lifting it into position.

STONE

While stone baskets of fruit are commonplace, baskets of flints are rather more unusual, but certainly no less attractive. Impressive containers can be filled with almost anything that appeals, so use your imagination and look beyond standard ideas.

Characteristics: Stone and reconstituted stone containers can be found in a wide range of designs, usually traditional, but sometimes modern. They range from heavily carved or modelled troughs and containers with a classical feel, to the utter simplicity of old stone sinks that were used for domestic purposes and for farm animals. While the first tend to look best in formal settings, the second will fit comfortably into less structured designs.

Slate water tanks were often used to collect rainwater, and if repaired make deep and wonderful containers, while some of the largest stone troughs, which were used for crushing cider apples, are large enough to contain a substantial collection of plants.

Uses: The classical patterns are at home in formal gardens, flanking entrances, acting as focal points, or helping to provide balance to a regular pattern of beds and borders. Any container is useful where there is no available open ground for planting, but should be as deep and generous as possible. Sinks and agricultural stone containers often provide a cool growing area for specialist collections of small plants such as alpines. Sinks can also become attractive small pools or water features, and some, originally used for juice extraction, have lips that will allow water to fall into another container below.

Construction: Reconstituted stone containers are cast from moulds, while natural stone is crafted by hand. Both require skilled labour.

Contrasting & associating materials: Both formal pieces and less formal sinks will relate well to natural stone or good quality precast concrete slabs, gravel, brick, along with grass and other soft landscaping.

Slate is a beautiful material that can be crafted into a vast range of different containers and patterns. Here the odd crack simply adds to the character of the piece, while the colour of the planting provides the perfect foil both to the slate and the white window and walls behind.

CERAMIC

These pots, with their distinctly Mediterranean influence, bring a splash of colour and a strong sense of movement to this setting and the bright planting has been chosen to suit their vibrant patterns. The containers have been raised from the ground to aid drainage.

Characteristics: Ceramic containers are becoming increasingly available, mostly from overseas, though there are several excellent English designers producing beautiful items. Chinese bowls are popular, as are those from the Mediterranean, but not all will be frost-proof. The beauty of ceramics lies in their surface patterning and colour, which can be dramatic or subtle. The larger containers will be free-standing, but smaller pieces are often designed to be hung on a wall. All pots must have a drainage hole, and it is a good idea to assist drainage on a paved area by standing them on specially moulded feet.

Uses: As their resistance to frost may be uncertain, it may be sensible to move these containers inside the house or conservatory during the winter. This being so, you could plant them with non-hardy species that will flourish outside in summer. As with any container, the larger the better, and a lightweight soil mix will make moving them easier.

Construction: This is a craftsman potter's job, and the higher the firing temperature the more durable the pot will be.

Contrasting & associating materials: Brightly coloured ceramics are vibrant and often look at their best in a contemporary design where other colours and different materials are freely used. If containers are hung on an outside wall, the wall (and continuous inside walls as well) could be painted to pick up the colour range of the containers.

Considerable thought has gone into co-ordinating this composition, and each element has been positioned with care and sensitivity. The deep blue glaze of the pots harmonizes perfectly with the ceramic tiles of the swimming pool.

TERRACOTTA

These wonderful organic shapes are placed over rhubarb to force the early stems into growth. They are almost too handsome to be hidden away in the vegetable patch and there is no reason why they could not be used to force rhubarb in more ornamental parts of the garden.

Characteristics: Terracotta has a long pedigree, and comes originally from the Mediterranean areas. One of the best-known and most popular materials for pots and containers, its clay base allows it to be moulded to virtually any pattern. Pots, troughs, window boxes and urns can all be found, with some urns commanding high prices at auction. With age, terracotta acquires a distinct patina that adds to its charm. I have pots of this kind that have been in use for over twenty years, the odd chip simply adding to their character.

Some of the finest containers come from Crete. These *pithoi* were originally storage jars, but are now increasingly made for export.

Uses: The natural colours of the clay make terracotta an ideal foil for planting, and as a rule, the larger the pot the happier the plants will be. They will have a cool root-run and the soil will dry out less quickly. Beware of plastic imitations that,

apart from being aesthetically dishonest, do not have the same cooling influence. The largest pots or urns can look effective if they are left unplanted and used as a focal point at the end of a vista or path. Smaller pots, of the same or varying size, look delightful set in groups on a paved area or flight of steps.

Construction: If you are a potter, you can throw your own. There are marvellous garden pots being made, most of which are manufactured in Mediterranean countries. Always check with suppliers that they are frost-proof. If they are not, they will crack and flake away in cold, damp winters. If in doubt, bring them indoors or swathe them in straw or bubble plastic during the winter.

Contrasting & associating materials: Terracotta is an extremely adaptable material, and will look equally at home in a mellow courtyard, formal garden or contemporary setting.

Terracotta becomes more and more beautiful with age. This superb urn was once painted, and the peeling surface only adds to its character. Raising an ornament to eye level often has the effect of throwing it into sharper relief, thus increasing its impact.

PRECAST CONCRETE

Concrete can be cast and finished in an extraordinarily varied range of finishes. This large pot has been cast in situ straight on to a base of stone, which it closely resembles.

Such a deep pot will provide ample room for a plant to spread out its roots, and if it is sited in a lightly shaded place should not require very frequent watering.

Shallow containers make the perfect choice for a selection of alpine plants, as many species appreciate the dry conditions that are usually created as a result of this type

of design. In this example, the pale colour of the concrete provides a pleasing contrast to the darker grey of the railway sleepers on which the container is standing.

Characteristics: Concrete is one of the most versatile materials in the garden, and as it can be cast into virtually any shape or pattern, it can also be used for pots and containers. These may be huge, such as sections of large-diameter drainpipe, which can be used as raised beds, right down to small bowls of the simplest design. Excellent examples of containers cast *in situ* can be found on the European continent and on the west coast of the United States, where they are often used to extend other hard landscaping such as walls or buildings.

Surface textures can vary, according to the type of aggregate selected, from a smooth, virtually polished finish, to one in which the aggregate in the mix is exposed to provide a rough and marbled finish. Ribbed and moulded patterns are also possible. As with anything to do with design, the character of the material should be respected; there is little point in using concrete to ape another material, though concrete quickly weathers down to resemble natural stone.

Uses: For plants, water, or as focal points. Containers cast *in situ* can be used as extensions to a terrace, to flank the edge of a hard landscape area, or to extend the line of a well-detailed flight of concrete steps in a contemporary setting. They would also be a logical choice to extend the line of a house built from concrete out into the surrounding landscape.

Construction: *In situ* containers will require wooden or ply shuttering, and skilled help. Most moveable containers will be bought from manufacturers or garden centres. The deeper and wider the pot, the better for planting.

Contrasting & associating materials: Although concrete is a contemporary material, it will blend into a wide range of settings depending on the style of design. As a general rule, concrete pots will look most comfortable within a crisp contemporary setting alongside precast concrete paving, railway sleepers and gravel.

METAL

Plain metal buckets make terrific containers and have an unfussy, clean appearance that will not detract from your chosen planting. Drill a few holes in the base of new buckets for drainage – older buckets may already have rusted through.

Lead is a particularly beautiful material, which looks better and better as it weathers, and this fine old lead sink bears a date and the initials of the original owner. As the container is so large, the planting should not require constant watering.

Characteristics: Metal is a versatile material and has considerable potential for containers in the garden. Historical pieces were often made from beautifully crafted lead, rich with patterning, and often bearing the coat-of-arms of the garden owners, together with the date. But there are some stunning contemporary designs being produced in all kinds of different metals and finishes.

Many metal containers will have started life as something else: copper or cast iron washing boilers are large and practical, simply needing holes drilled in the bottom for drainage, while coal scuttles, iron or copper, make smaller but useful pots. Old bathtubs, galvanized buckets (which are sometimes painted to imitate those used on barges), milk churns, old cattle or horse mangers, and bowls of various kinds, will all be suitable. Remember that very often the pot becomes incidental to the plant or plants in them, and it will be the plants that are the real stars.

Uses: For plants, or sometimes used empty as a dramatic focal point. A large, sound container can be used for a water feature.

Construction: Invariably a skilled metal-working job. Repairs will need to be carried out by an experienced blacksmith or welder.

Contrasting & associating materials: Fine old lead cisterns will be perfectly at home in a formal garden with traditional materials, while contemporary designs will look fine in a far more hi-tech situation, possibly combined with plastics, fibreglass and other crisp, visually clean surfaces such as railway sleepers or decking. As usual, match the container to the situation.

TIMBER

Large timber boxes of this kind can be bought in pieces and then assembled and positioned in the garden. Their ample proportions allow even rampant climbers to be grown, but once filled with soil, such containers will be difficult to move.

Characteristics: Timber is one of the most easily worked materials, and so the range of containers is almost limitless. Classical patterns, such as Versailles tubs, have a long history, and are perfect for a formal garden, while an old half-barrel, painted black and white, is ideal by the front door of a cottage. Colour, as well as protecting the surface can be used to link with an overall theme, or with overhead beams or decking. Window boxes bring plants into the vertical plane, and their use is often the only gardening option open to flat or apartment dwellers. As timber is relatively light, when filled with an equally lightweight soil mix it makes an excellent choice of container for a balcony or roof garden. Timber swells when wet, sealing construction joints, so containers can be used to form miniature water gardens.

Uses: As plant containers, herb and water gardens of variable size.

Construction: Timber is easily worked and can be tailored to fit awkward situations such as window openings or alcoves. Hardwoods are more durable than softwoods, but the latter can be pressure-treated prior to purchase, or regularly treated with a non-toxic preservative.

Contrasting & associating materials: Timber obviously has an affinity with other woodwork , whether this be decking, overheads, or raised beds built from railway sleepers. The potential of paint colour opens up possibilities for both harmony and sharp contrast with a surrounding scheme. As a rule, timber is a forgiving material, blending easily into a wide range of situations.

PLASTIC & FIBREGLASS

This arresting fibreglass pot makes a terrific statement, and proves that when treated in an innovative way, even the most mundane subject can become a major focal point. Choosing planting for such a pot might present quite a challenge.

Characteristics: Plastic and fibreglass are among the most misused and abused materials of the twentieth century. They have enormous potential for creating fresh organic shapes in wonderful colours, but that very versatility is so often used only to imitate other surfaces.

Any material should be used honestly and with integrity; to create a fibreglass pastiche of an old lead cistern, or a fine classical stone urn in plastic, is visually outrageous and aesthetic sacrilege. Synthetics are strong, rot-proof and virtually indestructible. Used properly, they can be an asset; used improperly, they are merely an environmental problem. The real strength of these materials is that they can be moulded in the widest range of shapes, particularly fluid and free-form patterns. Colour is no problem, from subtle pastels to vibrant primaries. Pots can be made in virtually any size,

often designed to stack or interlock together. They can be used either at ground-level, as window boxes or hanging containers, as well as for planting or for water, for which, being rot-proof, they are ideal.

Uses: For the widest range of pots and containers in contemporary designs. Naturally forming focal points, they are suitable either for plants or water. The material is light so is useful where load-bearing is a problem, particularly on roof gardens.

Construction: Moulded by specialist manufacturers. Unless you are an expert in the manufacture of fibreglass, these are items you will purchase.

Contrasting & associating materials: Almost exclusively for a contemporary setting, along with crisp, modern materials.

CAST & WROUGHT IRON

This highly detailed, matching set of garden furniture has a wonderfully regal air about it. Metal can be a cold material to sit on, but a few cushions will help to soften the outline in more temperate weather, perhaps co-ordinated to link with a colour scheme inside the house, as well as providing much needed comfort.

The combination of wrought iron and metal mesh in these garden rocking chairs is a fine example of traditional and contemporary techniques coming together in a way that is thoroughly practical and visually attractive. The colour blends perfectly into the garden and the seats will certainly be comfortable to sit in.

Characteristics: Cast iron furniture was made popular by the Victorians, who produced a vast range of patterns, styles and sizes. Pieces were often made in sections and then bolted together, sometimes entirely of iron, but often with slatted timber backs and seats. Such items are heavy, which gives them visual and actual stability, but chairs can be incredibly uncomfortable and often need cushions. Today, reproduction cast iron furniture is often made in alloy, making it lighter and less susceptible to corrosion.

Wrought iron is far more fluid in appearance, being made from strips of metal that are then joined together. Those wonderful park benches, where the ends and arms are wrought from a single spiral of material, look terrific in any garden. Designs can be infinitely varied, but try them for comfort before you buy. Tables often have wrought iron bases, and timber, glass or even marble tops. It all depends on how ostentatious you want to be! Heavy-gauge bent wire is also used for items of furniture, but tends to look flimsy. I don't like it!

There are some very beautiful modern designs being created today, so keep your eyes open. The metal is usually painted, which can link with a colour scheme used elsewhere. Avoid white, which gets dirty quickly and glares in sunlight.

Uses: For tables, chairs, benches and incidental items. Benches and seats often make ideal focal points, and can be positioned accordingly.

Construction: All metalworking is a skilled job, cast items coming from a foundry, and wrought iron from a blacksmith. Blacksmiths may also carry out repairs or make items to order. Maintain metal by rubbing down and repainting.

Contrasting & associating materials: Metal furniture can be modern in design, as well as traditional, and should be chosen accordingly to blend with the overall design. Don't be seduced by fashion, or what the neighbours have, unless you really like it and it suits your garden.

This elegantly shaped and beautifully designed metal furniture sits perfectly in a contemporary roof garden to provide an excellent example of modernism at its simple best. The neat flooring, monotone planting and finely detailed screen designed to filter the force of the wind, all combine to provide a well sheltered outdoor living space.

TIMBER

Timber is the most versatile of materials, and is relatively straightforward to work with. It can be shaped to a wide range of patterns, left plain or painted, and may either be freestanding or built directly into position. The neat and elegant design of this circular table and matching benches echo the white-painted house behind.

This stylish bench would fit comfortably into a wide range of situations, both architectural and informal, while the paint colour could be varied to suit alternative sites. The delicate and geometric design of the back slats blend particularly comfortably with the attractive tracery of branches in the background.

Characteristics: Apart from rocks, timber would have been the first material used by man for seating, and today the majority of furniture is still made from wood. The reason is simple: it is easily worked in a wide range of patterns and styles, is available in different types including hard- and softwood, and is relatively cheap. Other advantages are that it is mellow in colour and therefore does not glare in the sun, and that it ages gracefully, often with a beautiful patina.

Styles are legion, and include sets of tables and chairs, individual chairs, picnic tables with built-in seats, recliners and benches. Benches always amuse me: why do manufacturers make uncomfortably crowded three-seaters? Two-seaters are cosier, and often have a neat proportion that is not present in their larger cousins. Some designs are classic, the famous Lutyens bench being one of them. Such a seat is intended more as a focal point than a working sitting space. Humorous seats abound, with back-to-back lovers' seats and wheel-away barrow seats providing visual and practical fun.

I find much garden furniture, in whatever material, incredibly uncomfortable to sit on, so do try it out before you buy.

Uses: Often used as focal points as well as for practical purposes.

Construction: Timber is easily worked, and although you can buy sets, or single items of furniture, a competent carpenter can also make them. Both hardwood and softwood will need regular applications of preservative, or painting. You can also make basic rustic furniture out of fallen timber, although this tends to have a relatively short life and looks at its best in an informal setting. Entire tables and chairs can be cut out of single trunks with a chain saw, and these will last almost indefinitely.

Contrasting & associating materials: The enormous range of styles and colours available means that wooden furniture can be chosen to blend into virtually any situation.

Simplicity is the key to the success of these benches. Black is always an excellent choice of colour as it is relatively undemonstrative and tones well with planting as well as most hard landscape materials. This type of furniture will fit into virtually any surroundings.

STONE & RECONSTITUTED STONE

PLASTIC

The delicacy of this flower emphasizes the rugged nature of the simple granite seat, which has been formed from three pieces of stone. The weighty slab set in front of the bench is of practical benefit, saving wear on grass or other soft surfacing.

Characteristics: Stone has long been used for outdoor furniture, either in heavily patterned classical designs, or very simply conceived with blocks for legs and slabs for tops. Shapes for seats can be curved or rectangular, while tables are also often circular. The simplest and most effective of seats can be simply made from a single smooth rock, set with care in a particular place; once in position it will be difficult to move, so it is important to get it right first time! Natural stone (which can include sandstone, slate, marble, granite, and many more) is often very expensive, but infinitely variable and with superb coloration.

Reconstituted stone is popular, and far cheaper than the real thing. The best manufacturers faithfully reproduce classical designs. More imaginative contemporary pieces tend to be far less common.

Uses: Stone furniture is hard on the eye and hard to sit on, but can make a wonderful visual statement at the end of a walk, pergola or vista. Since the designs are almost always classical in inspiration, stone furniture is usually best in a formal or classical setting.

Construction: Natural stone is usually carved or shaped by craftsmen. Reconstituted stone is cast in moulds using specialist mixes, and is again usually a craft job.

Contrasting & associating materials: Classical or traditional pieces belong in similar settings, where natural stone paving, brick, gravel, grass and planting provide the ideal backdrop. Contemporary pieces, if you can find them, will associate with any of the above, but also concrete, precast materials, and timber, in the form of railway sleepers or decking.

Well-conceived plastic-coated metal furniture can be both practical and hardwearing. These chairs have a distinctly fifties feel about them, and would certainly be comfortable to use. The accompanying marble-topped table complements the seats.

Characteristics: As long as plastic furniture is designed to look like plastic, it is perfectly valid; as soon as it imitates something else, it is immediately degraded. Plastic is a naturally fluid material and is at its best when moulded into shapes that exploit this characteristic. The best quality furniture will last for many years, and although more expensive, is usually worth the extra cost.

Advantages include lightness, durability, which allows most sets to remain outside throughout the year, and the wide range of colours in which the furniture is made. White (the commonest colour) is best avoided; it not only glares in strong sun, but shows dirt easily. Most furniture of this type benefits from cushions, and these can be chosen to pick up a colourway inside the house.

Uses: Simply as furniture.

Construction: Moulded by specialist processes, plastic is sometimes also used as a protective coating to other materials such as metal, when, if carefully done, the finish can be both durable and attractive.

Contrasting & associating materials: Plastic furniture undoubtedly looks best in a contemporary setting, with materials to match.

HAMMOCKS

This free-standing hammock is supported on a elegantly minimal frame, and should be light enough to move around the garden at will. A stand is especially useful for gardens without any suitable trees. It should be a straightforward matter to remove the fabric from the frame for cleaning or replacement.

Characteristics: Hammocks provide the simplest and one of the most comfortable ways of relaxing in the garden, though they are far from easy to get in and out of; perhaps this is why you tend to spend a whole afternoon in a hammock, rather than just the five minutes you promised yourself! Canvas was the traditional material for hammocks, but this has largely been superseded by synthetics that are far more durable. The best hammocks use ample material, and come in a variety of open-mesh weaves as well as closely woven sheets. Most are still slung at will between two stout trees, but some up-market models now come complete with their own heavy stand. While these are useful for treeless town gardens and do away with the need for trees with stout trunks, the stands can be difficult to move.

I don't really mind about colour, it's comfort that is the most important factor, but if I had to choose, I would stick to cream. A few well-chosen cushions are essential.

Uses: Relaxation, mostly for people, but cats also love them. There can be few things better than gently swinging over the long grass of an orchard in the dappled summer sun.

Construction: Secure supports are essential; a fall can be painful and dangerous. Two strong trees are probably the best choice, although you could use bolts securely fixed to sturdy posts or walls. The hammock itself should always be regularly checked for wear, and ropes or fabric replaced as necessary. This is a feature that you could certainly make yourself.

Contrasting & associating materials: If you want to be ultra-sensitive, the materials could blend with others used elsewhere. I'm not too worried! An informal setting is best.

CANVAS

In my view, one of the greatest benefits of creating a beautiful garden is the pleasure obtained by relaxing in it. This scene has terrific charisma that has been achieved by combining a few simple elements: an old carpet flung on the terrace in the shadow of a fine tree, with canvas cushions tumbled around it. The view beyond is pure magic!

Characteristics: Canvas is a laid-back, easy-going material that always seems to smack of holidays by the sea, or picnics on the lawn. This is probably entirely due to childhood memories, but these things stick, which makes them all the more attractive. The material is surprisingly tough, is available in a wide range of colours and designs, and can be used for awnings, parasols, or chairs, of which the best known are deckchairs and so-called directors' chairs. Both types fold up for easy storage.

Awnings and parasols have gained in popularity over the past few years, and parasols are now made in a variety of sizes, the largest able to shade a considerable area. Most have adequate methods of anchorage, but this is obviously an important consideration. Unlike the gaudy floral affairs that used to be the only kind available, many awnings and parasols now come in an undemonstrative buff or cream that blends well into most settings.

Beanbags also make terrific garden furniture, for dogs as well as people, and are easily made up at home using waterproofed canvas and polystyrene beads. The rule is, the bigger the better.

Uses: Chairs and beanbags for sitting, awnings and parasols for shade. As all are made from fabric, the possibilities with colour are considerable. This is an area where you can really inject instant and immediate interest, and then remove it just as easily.

Construction: Chairs hinge and fold in various ways, the framework normally being timber. Although it is usually best to buy them, they are not impossible to make, if you have the time and patience. The canvas, or now rather more often, woven polyester, does wear over a period of time, and can usually easily be stripped off and re-tacked, stapled, or clamped back in place.

Canvas makes an excellent material for awnings, and these may be as straightforward as a single sheet cast over the branches of a tree, overhead beams or some other kind of framework, or as complicated as a specially manufactured structure that is rolled on a spring-loaded frame screwed on to the house wall. Parasols involve rather more intricate moving parts that slide up and down a central pole. This makes them relatively difficult to construct yourself. The material is usually stitched in position over the framework, and is similarly complicated.

Contrasting & associating materials: As with soft furnishings in the house, canvas garden furniture should be bought to blend with the setting; on the terrace, it will have a strong link with the interior of the house, so colours should be chosen with care. Apart from this, canvas furniture looks happily at home nearly anywhere in the garden: on a lawn, beside a pool, or within the shelter of a summerhouse.

Deckchairs are the most practical of chairs for storing and carrying around the garden. They are also extremely comfortable, and the fabric is easy to remove for cleaning or replacement. Be cautious about allowing children to put them up or down as fingers are easily trapped.

This composition has a wonderfully moody atmosphere! The unusually coloured parasol makes a perfect link with the colour of the building behind, and has been carefully positioned over the most sheltered of sitting areas.

MIRRORS

At first glance it is almost impossible to tell that there is a mirror set behind this arch, and the effect should succeed in fooling anyone who enters the garden for the first time. The result in this small town courtyard is the illusion of greater space.

Characteristics: With their obvious potential for increasing the size of an area in the most subtle way, mirrors are the small-space gardener's friend. It is worth dispelling one myth immediately: many people worry that birds will fly into them, with unhappy results. It is far more likely that a bird will try to fly 'through' a window than into a mirror, and I always ensure that there is ample foliage growing over the feature. This in turn enhances the effectiveness of the device.

The secret of using a mirror successfully lies in subtlety: there is little point in placing one four-square at the end of a path or vista, as you will simply see yourself getting rapidly larger as you approach it! The answer is to angle it slightly, preferably so that it reflects an area of planting, which will seem to recede into the distance. It is all down to double takes, and a mirror placed with skill really will deceive you.

In practical terms, the larger the reflective area the better the effect, and one of the most telling tricks is to place a mirror just behind a water slide or fall, when the stream seems to recede forever. Another similar trick is to angle a false door or archway slightly, so that it looks as if the approaching path leads into another garden room.

Humour can play an important part here. I once found a number of fairground distorting mirrors, and positioned them in various key points in a client's garden. Not only were they irresistible to the children, but they were a star attraction at parties, providing endless fun and ribaldry, which usually intensified as the evening wore on!

Uses: As a visual trick and often a major focal point. Mirrors really do engender a feeling of space, and if used with sensitivity are a worthwhile design tool.

Construction: The cheaper the better. Even if the mirrors are in poor condition, with the silvering breaking up, this really does not matter, as the whole thing will be surrounded and partially covered by planting. I'm always on the look-out for old wardrobe mirrors, or any discarded mirrors. Your local dump may be a fertile hunting ground, as, too, are junk shops.

Any mirror should be fixed securely for safety, and because breaking a mirror is supposed to bring bad luck. Most will be set within a timber frame that can be drilled and subsequently screwed to a wall. Mirrors can also be made by vacuum-coating polyester, and these are often available from shopfitting companies. They are light, and as they do not use glass, perfectly safe.

Contrasting & associating materials: Mirrors can go anywhere, and it is up to the skill of you or your designer to make them work effectively; they quite simply reflect everything around them.

MOSAICS

This most elegant of green rooms is filled with colour and textural interest. The seats are both delightful and durable, and you could have a great deal of fun choosing colour co-ordinated cushions. The floor is gorgeous and echoes the dramatic walls at a higher level, while the free-standing furniture has also been well-chosen.

This is a relaxed and clever arrangement that really works, demonstrating how drama can be used to create stunning effects. Vibrant colour makes a strong design tool, and this mosaic bench matches the wall perfectly. The tangled planting with its wayward roots has become an integral element of the overall pattern.

Characteristics: The golden age of the mosaic was in Roman times, when both floors and walls, inside and outside the home, were often worked with great skill and panache. Mosaic is characteristically built up from small pieces of coloured and glazed tile, either specifically made for this purpose, or from broken fragments. The work is carried out in much the same way as a painting, except that the individual pieces, of which there may be many thousands, are stuck in position. Today, the mosaic is undergoing something of a revival, and as a garden feature it has great potential, both in terms of visual appeal and of durability.

Uses: As a decorative element on the floor or walls. Mosaic can be used to line a summerhouse, a grotto, or a swimming pool; the best examples create stunning pictures or designs, not just a bland application of a single colour throughout.

Construction: If you have a creative eye, you may well be able to undertake the design and construction yourself; if not, there are a number of artists who specialize in the field. As the end result is exceptionally durable, make sure that you choose or create a pattern that you like; it will be visually demanding, and with you for a long time!

Pieces of mosaic about 12mm/½in sq are first assembled in large batches of the same colour. The pattern or picture is drawn out on the wall or floor before work starts, and the individual pieces are then either set in a cement grout or applied with a waterproof adhesive. Once the work is complete, the joints, which should be as small as possible, are finished by grouting the entire surface. It is of course essential that the vertical or horizontal surface to which they are applied is perfectly sound, and that the mosaic is constructed from materials that are frost-proof.

Contrasting & associating materials: Mosaics are highly individualistic, but can be designed to blend into either a classical or contemporary setting, with materials to match.

MURALS

Characteristics: Wall paintings, or murals, are part of our garden and architectural history; and they, like mosaics, are enjoying something of a revival. Attempts at realism will be rather more obvious than the effects achieved by mirrors, but are anyway usually intended to be evocative or amusing, rather than realistic.

Humour is again an almost essential ingredient, and the scene can be anything from a painted window that looks out over an idyllic landscape to a view of a Mediterranean harbour, to a false door engendering a feeling of space and the impression of a room beyond, or a purely abstract pattern designed to be appreciated as art.

Murals are particularly effective in town gardens, which are often surrounded by high walls, with little space for planting. What planting there is, can be reinforced by painted plants, if necessary of a similar kind, at a higher level. Arbours and vistas can be created with false perspective. I have even painted a low false wall on a high wall, complete with walking cat and barbecue, with wisps of painted smoke! Graffiti is considered a social crime, but the best examples are an art form of the highest order. In a hi-tech garden it could provide a fine contribution.

Uses: As visual trickery, to engender humour and a possible feeling of greater space.

Construction: By professional artists, or by amateurs; children are particularly good at both thinking up ideas and implementing them. Murals are usually painted on to rendered walls of a neutral colour, but are also sometimes seen on fences or on the sides of buildings. They can make terrific additions to the street scene.

Contrasting & associating materials: This depends entirely on the style and situation of the mural.

This incredibly stylish mural is pure escapism that indulges deliciously in the surreal. The misty grey colour scheme tones beautifully with the surrounding walls and paving and, while such a scene will fool nobody, it would make an intelligent addition to a wide range of outside spaces, especially those on a smaller scale.

TROMPE L'OEIL

This is trompe l'œil *on the grandest scale, in a garden combining classical columns, bold planting and a glimpse of trellis in the background. Such a device will set up different perspectives and create a feeling of greater space. The play of sunlight across the greenery provides dappled shade that will swing across the garden through the day.*

Characteristics: *Trompe l'œil* is designed to deceive the eye; the fact that it usually doesn't, matters little. It is simply one of those humorous devices that are purely for fun, adding another visual trick to many a tiny garden.

The effect is usually achieved by an arrangement of trellis, mounted on the surface of a wall and designed to look like an arch or tunnel receding into the distance. The trellis is often painted to allow it to stand out more effectively from the background. The centre section may contain a mirror, door, or window, and planting is often run over and around the feature to add to the effect. Occasionally a mural painting of a view is used. Such designs are usually traditional in spirit, but you may find a designer who is creating contemporary versions.

At its best this can be a delicate and well-conceived idea, cleverly woven into the rest of the garden fabric; at its worst, it is slapped on as an afterthought, when it is likely to end up being of little visual or aesthetic value.

Uses: As a visual trick to deceive, or at least humour the onlooker. It will naturally form a focal point, and can often be used at the end of a long narrow space or opposite a window or door inside the house. Pots, statues or other ornaments are sometimes placed to either side to provide additional emphasis.

Construction: *Trompe l'œil* is usually made from trellis, although metal or wire is sometimes chosen. The arrangement is screwed to a wall, often with a mirror similarly mounted in the middle. You can buy such features from up-market garden centres or specialist trellis manufacturers. Landscape companies will also build them to order. Maintenance will include painting or regular applications of a non-toxic preservative.

Contrasting & associating materials: This is a feature for a formal or classical garden, usually small and often in town. That being the case, surrounding materials should match, and could include natural stone, gravel, grass, containers, and a surround of leafy planting.

Experimentation and a choice of unusual subjects is the key to successful trompe l'œil. *This composition is unique to the owner, and a great feeling of depth is formed by looking past the statue, through the circle and into the garden beyond.*

TOPIARY

Characteristics: The art of topiary, and it is very much an art, dates back thousands of years. The skill is to clip or train virtually any kind of plant material into almost any kind of artificial shape. These can generally be divided into architectural shapes (cubes, cones, obelisks, balls, arches) and virtually any other shape (animals of every conceivable and humorous kind, as well as trains, ships, houses, cars, planes and so forth). Quite simply, the sky is the limit.

In the United States and certain other parts of the world, creeping plants, such as *Ficus pumila*, are also used to create a variety of sculptural shapes. These are grown into and over a wire framework stuffed with moss, which allows an even greater range of intricate shapes and patterns to be built up than could be achieved by clipping.

Spirals are one of the most commonly used shapes in topiary and can be straightforward to achieve. Box, used here, is one of the best plants to use as it is so simple to clip and train. The accompanying ivy softens the outline of the bowl, but care should be taken to keep it in control.

Topiary can be used *en masse* in serried ranks or as a single statement; the scale huge or diminutive; the subject serious or funny; the setting formal or informal: the choice is yours! But perhaps the most important thing is that such shapes can be created by anyone with just a little, or a lot, of imagination.

Uses: Very much as living sculpture, and almost invariably as some kind of focal point to draw the eye. Both choice and positioning have infinite possibilities; the only real limitation is the ultimate characteristic of the species involved, and the need to plant it in a position where it can develop without visually swamping the immediate area.

Construction: This is the skilled part of the job. Much topiary uses slow-growing and dense hedging plants such as yew or box (though many other plants can be also be used). An individual plant is usually trained around some kind of framework that will outline the shape required. The branches will be carefully tied into the frame, and clipped so that the form slowly takes shape. The process may take a couple of seasons or many years, depending on the size and complexity of the finished article. The frame is often removed once the shape is complete, and any further trimming will depend on the eye of the gardener. (It has to be said that strange mutations sometimes develop after a while!) For simpler shapes, such as an obelisk or lollipop, the plant is often allowed to grow up freely, with or without a stem, and trimmed against a template when the time comes. As with any heavily pruned plant material, regular feeding is essential.

Contrasting & associating materials: This will depend on the style of the piece. Geometric shapes in a fine old garden will look perfect set among sweeping lawns and gravel paths, while something far more contemporary, and perhaps humorous, will look at home in a hi-tech setting of concrete, decking, and precast paving.

Topiary on a large scale is an art form, albeit one that requires careful and regular maintenance. There is considerable rhythm and movement in this composition, *that draws the eye down the central path and on into the garden beyond the archway. Gravel makes an excellent foil to clipped plants.*

DECORATIVE PLANT SUPPORTS

These decorative ceramics provide a delightfully light-hearted and practical safeguard against the dangers of poking your eye on the top of a sharp stick. Before placing this type of object in the garden, always check that it is completely frost proof – it would be a great shame to lose such fun objects in the cold winter months.

Characteristics: Time was, when the only support for your plants would be a collection of bamboo canes or twiggy branches. Today this has changed, and the herbaceous border plays host to all kinds of clever devices that expand and grow in height along with the plants. There is also a trend to make a feature of supports for plants that can be persuaded to climb, and various trellis-work or metal arrangements are now available, usually shaped like some form of obelisk. These are either set on their own feet in a border, or placed in boxes, similar to Versailles tubs, as a focal point. Such supports are highly stylized, but where trellis or other metal features are already present in the garden, their use can be very effective. The colour of the supports can be linked to that of timber- or metalwork elsewhere.

There are, of course, other decorative supports that can be fixed to walls. These are usually a variation of trellis or wattle, and will include fan and other geometric patterns. The visual value of these is dubious, and they invariably require a certain amount of regular maintenance.

Uses: Usually as a support for climbers, which can include all but the most rampant species. In a formal and decorative vegetable garden, they can become part of the overall pattern, and used for climbing vegetables or, decoratively, for roses or other climbing flowering plants. In a formal pleasure garden, they can be used in much the same way as you would use statuary or topiary, to flank a terrace, path or walk.

Construction: Either of trellis or metal, usually in the shape of an obelisk, with feet that can be pushed into the ground. If they are fitted to boxes, the boxes should be as large as sensibly possible, to allow good root development and reduce the amount of watering necessary. Features of this kind will probably demand skilled help.

Contrasting & associating materials: Almost invariably in a formal setting, along with natural stone paving, brick, gravel paths and lawns. Alternatively, in a well-kept vegetable garden, where these materials will predominate.

This is a perfect example of a support becoming incidental to the planting, which is just how it should be. Such frames provide practical and elegant hosts to a wide range of scrambling and climbing plants, and are as suitable for climbing or runner beans as they are for ornamental plants.

LIGHTING

Lighting has literally changed the way in which we look at the garden, extending our enjoyment of it into the evening and night, providing security, and, at its best, enhancing the beauty of everything it illuminates. The fact that lighting is under-exploited and unimaginatively used is a great pity, as the potential of this infinitely variable medium is enormous.

Its use can be split broadly into lighting for practical reasons: to illuminate points of access, paths, driveways, utility areas and the immediate vicinity of the house; and lighting for purely decorative purposes. The problem is that the distinction between the two types has often been too rigid; a great deal of functional lighting can also be both subtle and decorative, though there is unfortunately still a plethora of poorly designed fittings on the market that rarely complement architecture or landscape.

Another problem is that lighting is so often not considered during the design stage of the garden, which means that its later installation may be extremely disruptive and fittings may not be chosen to blend with the overall style. The result can be a dangerous tangle of wires, leading to certain visual mayhem.

Lighting design is both sensitive and an important part of the garden as a whole. There can be little to commend setting old cast iron lamp standards, originally gas and now converted to electricity, up a leafy suburban drive. They were not designed for the purpose, would cost a small fortune to install, would contribute little to the garden, and would simply look ostentatious. The same principle applies to sticking imitation Georgian coach lamps on the facade of a

nineteen-fifties house; either is fine on its own, but together they are incongruous. It is important to think about these kinds of relationships.

Practical lighting should, of course, be that, but don't just think in terms of highly powerful halogen floodlights that drown out everything in the area. Such lighting can prove burglar-friendly; the surrounding areas of shadow seem so dark by contrast, that a person can be virtually invisible. Lower wattage lamps, carefully positioned and in sufficient number, can be both more effective and

a good deal easier on the eye. The lighting of a driveway, and other access routes, can be a beautiful affair; there are, for example, ranges of well-designed bollards or ground-level lights that can cast a wide, but again subtle beam, exactly where it is needed.

Steps and changes in level are always points where illumination is needed, and perhaps the most important point here is to make sure that the light is cast at a low level, rather than on the top of your head. One of the prime rules for any

These subtle lights provide both upward and downward beams from exceptionally discreet fittings on the pillars. This type of lighting produces a feeling of warmth rather than a harsh glare. The lighting within the swimming pool is equally low-key and effective.

kind of illumination is that the light is more important than the fitting. If possible (and this is a general rule of installing lighting in and around hard landscape features), try and recess the fitting into the structure. There are many lights that are designed to be built as part of the adjoining brickwork or the step riser.

Decorative lighting is an entirely different subject, and one where skill and a good eye come into play. There are a number of specialist lighting designers who ply their trade successfully, and it is no surprise that many of these were originally trained in the theatre, where the importance of using lights for subtlety and drama has long been recognized.

There are a number of rules that are worth remembering: a garden that is lit up like Blackpool or Coney Island is not only boring but vulgar; try to create a composition where not all is visible at one time. The coloured lights sold at garden centres (red, green and orange) look revolting, turning foliage and nearly everything else a sickly hue; instead, use white and blue lights that enhance rather than detract from everything around them. As sunlight is always cast from above, we get used to everything being top lit; with artificial lighting we can project a beam from wherever we want, and this provides a whole new dimension, particularly with planting, where the shape, texture and underside of foliage is rarely seen at its best.

The installation of any system should be approached with respect, even though many lighting systems are low-voltage. Instructions should be followed to the letter if you are doing the work yourself, with the correct transformers or circuit breakers fitted. If in any doubt over anything electrical in the garden, always enrol the help of a qualified electrician. If you do install your own system, have someone to help you, not just on the technical side, but to move fittings around to get the effect you want. This is of course a night-time job, and it should also be remembered that as a garden grows and changes, lights may well need to be repositioned.

This is a brilliant example of lighting design that is full of drama and makes a great addition to the scene. It perfectly fulfills the adage that less is much, much more, with its impeccably simple flooring, walls, planting and light. The invitation to step into the next garden room to enjoy yet more pleasures is virtually irresistible.

LIGHTING TECHNIQUES

Spotlighting: This is perhaps the best known method of lighting, and uses a concealed source, usually at a higher level, to pinpoint an object, usually a focal point, and throw it into sharp relief, contrasting it with the surrounding darkness. As the light is usually positioned some way away, the beam will need to be relatively powerful; if it is cast at a slight angle to the feature, it will cast shadows across the face, providing rather more interest than a head-on approach.

Backlighting: This is the reverse of spotlighting, and the light is positioned behind and relatively close to the object to be lit. The wattage is usually low, and the effect is to make the object glow, with the outline shimmering against the dark. This is precisely what happens in an eclipse, where the dark ring of the moon highlights the corona of the sun. If positioned and handled correctly it is one of the most telling of lighting methods.

Grazing: Not for cattle, but where a wide spreading beam, or number of beams, are placed at an angle at the bottom or top of a feature, often the face of a building, to allow the light to graze the surface and pick out all the texturing. The technique can work with most large objects, including statues, ornaments and focal points, and often allows detailing to be revealed that cannot be appreciated in daylight.

Uplighting: Here, a light is positioned below a particular feature or plant, often set into the ground, to throw the outline into sharp relief. It is particularly effective with individual trees in an expanse of lawn, where the sculpture of the branches can be breathtaking. A small spinney lit in this way provides high drama.

Moonlighting: Moonlighting has a number of connotations, but in terms of lighting it involves low-wattage bulbs set in a tree or large arbour.

A garden need not be lit with only one type of lighting; there is a whole variety of lights used here, all of which illuminate the features and planting using different techniques. The greatest sense of drama can often be achieved by allowing a great swathe of darkness to hang over the garden, emphasizing everything below.

These allow illumination to fall downwards through the structure, to cast shadows on the ground below. This is a magical technique that produces the most beautiful effects.

Underwater lighting: So often done poorly, but has enormous potential. Those rotating floating displays that dance on the surface and give you an instant migraine should be banned. Subtle underwater lights, in blue or white, can be positioned beneath fountains, waterfalls, bubble jets and statues with subtle and stunning effect. Streams and cascades can benefit, as well as millstones or boulder features.

Alternative lighting: As far as lighting technology for the garden is concerned, precious little seems to have happened since the invention of the light bulb. If we look at other areas of industry we see the most exciting innovations, some of which have already been with us for quite a time. Lasers, fibre optics and holograms are all in common use elsewhere, but the gardening fraternity, at its snobby worst, still persists in turning up its nose at them.

Goodness only knows why; they can provide the most subtle and stunning effects that I have used, continue to use, and hopefully also educate others to appreciate. Their installation can be complicated, and lasers in particular can be harmful if used incorrectly, but the results, in the right situation, can be unforgettable.

Nor does the technology stop there. Lighting can be linked to synthesizers for music and other background sound, as well as to a mechanical system of operating doors, overhead structures such as awnings and an ever-increasing number of other innovative items.

One day, things such as non-toxic atmospheric colorants will be produced, and you will be able to create your own personalized climatic zone; virtual reality will become an added tool to the garden palette. There is more to gardening that most of us ever think about; experimentation can only broaden our minds.

This spectacular display has been achieved using very simple and relatively cheap elements. Candles inside glass containers provide a highly effective means of lighting the way around the garden at night, where they may be used to flank paths or mark the edge of a paved area. The fireworks in the urns add a touch of instant, if short-lived, drama.

RESTORATION & MAINTENANCE

Growing old gracefully should be part of life, and one of the great attractions of a mature garden is the patina of age: a combination of fully developed planting, well-weathered hard landscape, well-worn incidental features that would include the rich verdigris of copper, the silver bleaching of wood or the natural lichens on a stone ornament, and the accretion of incidental features (statues, ornaments and general furnishings). Even gardens that are contemporary in style feel more comfortable when the shine has worn off, and the hard edges are softened by flower and foliage.

Some of the finest weathered objects are those that have been found by chance. I have in my own garden old sun-bleached logs that were found on a beach, an old copper coal scuttle and a broken down grinding stone, none of which require any maintenance, but all of which add immeasurably to the character of their surroundings. However, since gardens are living and changing entities, many of the features in them will begin to need attention as they age, to prevent them from decaying further, and to prolong their useful life. At the other end of the spectrum, ageing techniques may be required to mellow the components of a new garden and help it achieve a point of timeless perfection. Manufacturers today often age their new products artificially and sell them at a premium. There is nothing wrong in this, as long as they clearly state the fact, but it just proves the point that the patina of age is seen as a desirable additive.

You may also perhaps have inherited an old garden with elements that need restoration, or bought garden features that need the same. Objects in need of restoration often go cheaply at auctions – a fertile hunting ground for all kinds of garden goodies.

This cast iron urn was once painted but is now all the more attractive as a result of the rust acquired over many years. Cleaning up the container would lessen its appealing character, especially as the petunias look so fresh in contrast.

Here is the old man of the garden, partially hidden but far from forgotten. The accumulation of lichen and the softening influence of the foliage have provided him with a degree of dignity, but the plants will need to be cut back from time to time.

Restoration is a delicate path to tread, and as with other forms of art, there is always the question of whether to restore or not. Very often it will be better to leave things as they are; the natural character of a cracked urn or a chipped statue simply adding to its charm.

At the end of the day, it's the straightforward maintenance of a garden that pays the greatest dividends, and the routine tasks of combating wear and tear are just as important as the more specialized jobs mentioned above. One of the best pieces of advice is to carry out maintenance on a regular basis. Little and often makes sense in most areas of life, and especially in a garden if the whole thing is not to become a perpetual millstone round your neck.

Are these seats actually used or simply positioned here as an unusual focal point? This is irrelevant in visual terms, but if they are used they will need urgent attention to prevent them from falling apart! Very old, naturally weathered timber has great charm, and is difficult, but not impossible, to reproduce artificially.

RESTORATION TECHNIQUES

The need for restoration is very much a question of personal choice; minor damage to a statue, pot or ornament rarely detracts from its charm, and the same applies to railings, gates, paving, walls, buildings and any other features. On the other hand, if the feature has become dangerous, or is in danger of disintegration, some remedial work will have to be carried out.

The key to restoring anything is to assess the extent of the damage thoroughly before you start work, and the more complex the project the more important this is. Never rush in and start to chop out damaged sections of, say, a garden building before you have ascertained, in mechanical terms, just how the structure goes together; the result could be disastrous. Have supporting jacks and tools ready, waterproof sheets to cover any sections of exposed roof, and as much new material as you think necessary to hand, so that you are ready to start the restoration immediately.

If the work is likely to be extensive, always take photographs before you start, so that you can remember any pertinent details and reproduce them faithfully.

Skills needed will vary in difficulty according to the complexity of the item to be restored, and the nature of the material. Timber obviously calls for carpentry and joinery, and may require carving skills. Some, or all of this you may be able to tackle yourself. Alternatively, you may need to call on the services of a professional. New timber should match the original; hardwoods, for example, perform quite differently from softwoods in terms of expansion and contraction, as well as durability. Timber was traditionally well seasoned, which is not always true today, and the modern system of kiln drying is not so satisfactory. However, there are still small timberyards that offer seasoned wood, and they will often take a great interest in a specific restoration job.

The restoration of walling and paving usually requires careful but relatively straightforward work. Damaged and weathered material may need chopping out and replacing with new;

A cracked container can often be carefully repaired by drilling each piece, fitting short lengths of wire or rod, and sticking the whole thing together with waterproof adhesive.

pointing may need raking back and renewing; arches taking down and carefully rebuilding around a turning piece. It is important to save all useable materials that you take down, for possible re-use, and match any new materials as closely as possible. This may be the longest part of the job, but it's always worth the wait to track down the right thing.

Complicated stone restoration of highly decorated pieces is a job best left to the experts, as a crude attempt looks just that and will ultimately ruin the object. While I would not suggest that you tackle the repair of broken load-bearing columns, lintels or sills, on safety grounds, the professionals will certainly take them in their stride, drilling the various pieces and reassembling them using stainless steel dowels and specialist adhesives. Straightforward repairs of decorative stonework or reconstituted stone, can be undertaken by using crushed stone and sand mixed with cement. The colour of the former is critical and can sometimes be obtained

This bridge is probably still safe to walk across, but it has reached a point in life where restoration is necessary to prevent any further decay. Provided the supports into the water are still sound, the job should be achievable using only basic carpentry skills, although it may be difficult to find replacements for some of the longer timbers.

If this beam is load-bearing it will need renewal, otherwise it is probably best left as it is, as there is enormous character in the beautifully aged wood with its accumulations of lichen. So long as they are not actually dangerous, old structures are often best left alone as the stress caused by renovation can cause them to collapse.

This beautifully laid surfacing is the ultimate study in texture and pattern of now elderly hard landscaping materials. There is no need for any remedial work to be carried out here; all that is required is a respect for the craftsmen who did such a wonderful job.

from the original manufacturer or quarry. Stone or monumental masons may either be able to supply these materials or carry out the necessary work.

If terracotta pots are simply breaking up through frost damage, there is little you can do but breakages are a different matter. The strength of glues has increased enormously over the past few years, but Araldite is still one of the best. Surfaces should be cleaned and carefully drilled, if the thickness of material will allow, to enable thin metal dowels to be inserted. Adhesive is then applied to each surface, following the manufacturer's instructions, and the pot carefully reassembled before being held tightly together using a tourniquet while it dries.

The restoration of metalwork is a highly specialist job that is best left to a blacksmith, but it is often well worth removing a gate or section of fine old wrought or cast iron railing and getting the work done. Most craftsmen revel in the chance to restore items that were made by their same trade many years before, but do shop around to find someone that really understands the job, and always ask to see examples of their work first. Where an item cannot be removed, because of its size or permanence, then a craftsman may be able to visit the garden and carry out work on site.

As a final thought, remember that restoration is not only applicable to antique or old items; 'modern' materials such as concrete have been with us for a long time now. Even with a simple job like renewing the timber slats in a bench, or rebuilding a well-detailed flight of concrete steps, the rules are the same: take your time, assess the work involved, carry it out carefully and make sure, if you can, that the new work will last as long, if not longer, than the original.

SOURCING & MATCHING MATERIALS

Sourcing materials is enormous fun, and will take you far and wide to places you never thought existed. You could be looking for a row of a particular coping brick, a finial for the top of a garden house, a run of iron railings, lead flashing for the roof, bricks or stone, or simply a number of old paving stones.

Remember to save any original fixtures and fittings that you come across. These might include old hand-made nails, hinges, bolts, brackets, ironwork for tying structures together, and all

kinds of other things. It may even be worth having some of these items repaired, as replacements may be impossible to find, and it will be they that give the new work a sense of age. I have often been seduced into buying up odd objects of doubtful value that 'might come in one day', and that now lie in heaps waiting for a use!

You may well find York or other sandstone paving and materials at a garden centre, but the price will be high. Stone yards carry a vast range of different paving materials, and although they

usually deal with the trade they will normally provide a member of the general public with a reasonable quantity. Demolition yards are a fertile hunting ground for paving, timber, beams, edgings, copings, slates, tiles, bricks, stone, and almost anything else you can think of, but the owners caught on a long time ago to the value of almost anything. There are also an increasing number of specialist salvage yards, which are a step up from demolition merchants, and go under the rather more respectable name of architectural salvage. They are inevitably more expensive but usually better organized, and better geared to the general public. Professional landscape contractors often have a stockpile of ancient and worthwhile goodies, just waiting for the right job to come along, and they, too, can be well worth a visit. As with many businesses, cash talks volumes.

If you are matching materials, take a sample along with you. It's usually impossible to remember the exact colour and texture of a brick or other item, but place it alongside the new one and the job is made easy.

Half the fun of finding old things is the chance it provides to haggle about the price, so don't go shopping in your Sunday best; prices are usually negotiable, and most staff can see a soft touch coming a mile off. Always know what you are looking for, and try to have at least an approximate idea of the price you are prepared to pay. Listen to other people buying and then make your own negotiations. Be aware, too, of any potential problems, such as oil-stained York paving stones, or tar-covered railway sleepers, and ask the dealer where the materials came from. Inspect them closely, and only make your mind up when you are ready.

Auctions are another great place to find what you want, and these will vary enormously, depending on where they are in the country, the weather on the day, and how well known they are. Some of the top London auction houses hold sales of garden ornaments and statuary, but the prices will be high. Better to go to the smaller, less well-known affairs, or keep an eye on your local paper;

This type of fitting should always be saved for re-use once the structure it belongs to has reached the end of its useful life. Such fittings can either be incorporated into a replacement, *or used elsewhere. Oak always weathers down to a superb colour, and here it is heightened by the wonderful crimson of the sprawling rosehips behind.*

This Aladdin's cave full of old terracotta pots, is not only valuable, but the pots also have years of life left in them. Old pots always look more attractive than new ones, largely as a result of the change in coloration and the occasional cracked rim. Terracotta can be artificially 'aged' and the growth of lichen encouraged using methods explained overleaf.

The worth of recycling old objects which may be from another age and have been created for a different purpose is well illustrated by this wonderful old metal container, which has been used to make a striking water feature.

farm sales often turn up the most wonderful treasures at ridiculously low prices. Beware, too, of auction fever; it can be a disaster, and result in you coming away with a load of junk. Always go to the sale preview, and if you see something you like, look at it quite dispassionately and try to convince yourself you don't need it. Always have a firm ceiling price in mind, and resolve never to exceed it, even in the heat of bidding.

Antique shops are for the well-heeled; junk shops yield surprising treasures for the rest of us! But of course you don't always have to buy an antique. If you are looking for old stone ornaments or statues, there are a number of firms producing excellent reproductions that will soon weather down to look as old as you like. They often also sell off damaged 'seconds' that have been standing about for quite some time. Prices will vary, but they will all be considerably cheaper than antiques. Such firms are also able to copy existing objects, and while this is expensive, it may be worth considering if you are restoring an historic garden and want to match specific items. If you are looking for a new house and garden, always search diligently for unusual objects. The discovery of an old bench or pair of rotting wrought iron gates may not necessarily influence your choice, but once they have been reclaimed you will have the satisfaction of feeling that you have gained something for nothing.

As a final thought, always look out for the unexpected: a big old wardrobe mirror for the back of a border to give the illusion of space in a town garden; an old bathtub for a herb garden; pots and containers that started life as something else; or a pair of cast iron columns that would make wonderful supports for overhead beams. Very often the discovery of an object will be instrumental in influencing a whole new train of garden design. Go out and buy; have fun!

AGEING TECHNIQUES

Lichen takes a number of years to develop naturally, but the process can be accelerated by an application or two of an organic substance such as yoghurt. The richly textured colours of the lichen which has colonized this old brick wall, are reminiscent of a van Gogh painting.

Weathered boards always look superb although hardwoods will stand up to time better than softwoods. Part of the charm here lies in the slight irregularity of each slat and in the striking contrast of the pale boards with the vibrant colour of the Virginia creeper.

A rich patina of age is not only valuable in visual terms, but will often considerably increase the financial worth of an object. Many manufacturers of reconstituted stone keep a certain amount of stock aside to weather down, and this is then sold at a premium. You, however, can do exactly the same thing yourself, and to be fair, those same companies often sell a proprietary ageing compound that can be brushed on to the ornament or pot to accelerate its colonization by mosses and lichens.

Traditionally, liquid manure was slapped all over the object, which certainly did the trick but smelled revolting and had the added problem of attracting thick swarms of flies. You can in fact use anything organic: milk, stale beer, or yoghurt. Yoghurt is remarkably effective, and you will have a good surface texture after about six months; shady areas encourage the growths of moss and lichens more quickly than sunny spots.

The simplest and most effective way that I have found is simply to leave the piece in long grass for six months, turning it once or twice in the process. The organic treatment can be used for individual objects, for walls, and for most other things you want to age down. Paving of course is a different story; this must be kept clean if a dangerously slippery surface is to be avoided.

Timber can also be aged, and this can be useful for whole areas of decking, or if you need to weather down replacement boards. It is, incidentally, always worth keeping a number of boards aside when building a deck, and allowing these to weather down naturally.

The grain of any timber runs in lines down and through the boards, alternating between harder and softer wood. Professionals often dip boards in acid, which has the effect of exposing the harder grain, which is darker than the surrounding softwood. Acid, however, is a dangerous substance, and a far better way to age timber is as follows: select the number of boards you need, and carefully burn the surface with a blow lamp, just scorching the softwood, and leaving the hard grain exposed. Then wire brush down the length of the grain to remove the scorched surface of the softwood. Once that is done, the surface can be painted with watered-down white or grey emulsion paint, and wiped over with a cloth to clean the paint off the exposed grain, leaving it in the depressions. The effect, when dry, is close to that beautiful sun-bleached colour of weathered boards, and should last several years, by which time natural weathering will have taken over.

This technique can be used on a boarded or slatted fence, as well as for ageing the brash new timbers of a garden building.

You can also 'distress' timbers if you need to replace them, or if you are building a structure that has to blend into a traditional setting. Large beams were traditionally fashioned with a sharp hand-cutting tool called an adze, which imparted irregularities and an overall roughened surface. A similar effect can be obtained by using a large spokeshave or carefully wielded chisel, the surface being finally stained an appropriate colour to match the existing woodwork.

The real point with any ageing technique is to use it with sensitivity and only where it is appropriate. There is no point in doing it for its own sake; that is the prostitution of good design.

Some pieces have an in-built patina of age. Ceramic is especially suitable for this treatment as pigments and irregularities can be incorporated beneath the glaze.

This slightly menacing figure is a well-weathered and ancient piece that has gradually been covered with a combination of mosses, lichen and ivy. In many ways this example conveys the essence of good ornamentation: its positioning means that it looks comfortable within its surroundings, and it is rich with the charisma of old age.

MAINTENANCE

Maintenance is the key not only to keeping any garden under control, but to prolonging the life of many incidental features, and a modicum of time spent on routine tasks will save a great deal of hard work and expense in the long run. Like housework, garden work is best tackled on a regular basis, and certain jobs are easiest done at specific times of the year. Almost all garden materials require some degree of maintenance, whether paving, timber, metal, or special features and furnishings. Much maintenance is best undertaken in the winter, when any planting that covers, surrounds, or is positioned in front of a feature is likely to have died down.

Good-quality wrought iron is always worth preserving and regular attention in the form of rubbing down and repainting will be necessary. If you have a wrought iron gate, check that the posts are set firmly into the ground and oil the hinges at frequent intervals.

It is often arguable whether an object is best cleaned up or left to weather untouched, however, if you wish to prolong its life, the former action is essential. To preserve a wooden chair such as this it should be allowed to dry out before being rubbed down and treated either with a non-toxic preservative or a good coat of paint.

Materials should ideally be suited to the prevailing conditions. Timber, for instance, is not the best choice for deep shade, and in places where smooth paving becomes slippery, gravel, granite setts and ribbed concrete would be a better proposition.

The main problem associated with paving occurs in shady areas where the surface grows algae, making it slippery. Any paved area should be regularly brushed down to prevent a build-up of leaves and other debris, which will naturally get slimy, but if algae is a real problem you can use a proprietary patio cleaner or pool algaecide, remembering to keep these well clear of any plants. Alternatively, a good scrubbing down with soapy water will do the job almost as well. Timber may also become slippery, and a scrub down once a year should be enough to keep the surface clean.

Unpainted fences, wooden buildings, pergolas, arches and other timber surfaces should be treated annually against rot with a non-toxic preservative (never creosote, which is sure death to plants). Pay particular attention to where posts or boards are set into, or come close to the ground, as this is often the most vulnerable point. Any climbing plants should be carefully taken down (if they are trained on wires the task becomes a good deal easier), and tied back once work is complete. Painted surfaces should also be rubbed down and repainted on a regular basis. Gates will need oiling, and their alignment checked and rectified if necessary.

Glass structures such as greenhouses and cold frames, need regular attention. Glass is normally held in position with clips; these are easily dislodged so it is worth keeping a supply of spares at hand – readily obtainable from the manufacturer or supplier. Broken glass should *always* be replaced immediately. If a pane is missing, strong winds can cause air pressure to build up inside a greenhouse, and in extreme circumstances it can literally explode. Whereas the frameworks of metal greenhouses and cold frames are largely maintenance free, all timber structures are prone to rotting and should be treated regularly using a non-toxic preservative. Parts that have deteriorated badly should be cut out and replaced.

The closed environment of a greenhouse can encourage pests and diseases. There are many ways to tackle this, including biological control using predator insects known as nematodes. Sensible husbandry will include washing surfaces down and cleaning pots with a suitable general-purpose disinfectant. Soil may also need sterilizing but in recent times, the increased use of growing bags has reduced this chore considerably.

All garden chemicals should be kept in a locked cupboard and any old or unwanted ones should be disposed of safely: your local authority will normally have a facility for this.

Pools and water features will need a regular check over, but contrary to common belief should not be drained on an annual basis. If the pool is well stocked with fish, which produces a consequent build up of toxins, it is sufficient to drain off approximately a quarter of the volume, which will still retain the natural balance of the pool water, and replace with fresh. Ice on ponds can be a problem as it allows toxic gases to build up, which can be detrimental to fish and other pond life. The most basic solution is to float a ball or log on the surface, which will keep a small area clear of ice. Small, floating electric pool heaters can also be used; these are cheap to run and highly effective. If fallen leaves from overhanging trees are a problem, a fine mesh net can be positioned over the pool just before autumn. This should be emptied as necessary.

Pump filters should be cleaned every month or so, and any electrical fittings should be regularly checked over and replaced by a qualified person if there are any problems.

Hardwood timber furniture will need an annual rub down followed by an application of a preservative such as teak oil; boiled linseed oil is one of the best treatments for softwoods. Regularly maintained timber furniture should last for a very long time. Manufacturers rarely sell replacements for items such as broken bench slats, but a timber yard will almost certainly be able to match something up. Most repair work requires only basic carpentry skills; it should be possible to use old or broken sections of furniture as a template for replacement. Metal furniture should be rubbed down with a wire brush and repainted regularly. Broken metal furniture is virtually impossible to repair.

Waterproofed fabrics and awnings can be spray-protected with a suitable product, while barbecues, both built-in and free-standing, should be cleaned up prior to winter.

Garden tools, both manual and power-driven, should always be kept sharp, clean and in good running order. Larger tools such as lawnmowers should be serviced by professionals. Sharp and potentially dangerous equipment must be kept well out of the reach of children.

The repair of garden lighting systems, apart from renewing bulbs, is a job for a qualified electrician. However, it is worth checking rubber seals, cables, plugs, sockets and fittings for signs of wear. For safety, always use a circuit breaker, and if there is a fault, switch off the circuit.

Large ponds will not require a great deal of attention so long as they are well stocked with oxygenating plants and fish, but a net should be cast over the surface in autumn to catch most of the falling leaves. The statue here adds the finishing touch to this delightful composition.

AGGREGATE
The small stones in a concrete mix that may be exposed by brushing when the concrete is still damp to form a textured finish.

ARRIS RAILS
The horizontal rails set between morticed posts on to which vertical fence boards are nailed.

BATTER
The upward and inward incline commonly used when building dry stone walls to provide additional strength.

BUTT-JOINTED
A method of laying paving slabs or any other materials in which slabs are laid tightly together without any joints.

COTSWOLD STONE
A honey-coloured sandstone frequently used in Great Britain.

CREASING COURSE
A single or double course of tiles or slate set beneath a coping of brick set on edge.

DAMP PROOF COURSE
A strip of bitumen roll set just above ground level in brick walls to prevent rising damp.

EXPANSION JOINT
A narrow vertical joint incorporated in long runs of walling to allow for expansion and contraction.

FEDGE
A hybrid between a fence and a hedge, usually a framework covered with wire on to which climbing or scrambling plants can be trained.

FEEDER POOL
A pool, usually at the bottom of a stream or waterfall, from which water is recirculated by means of a pump.

FOOTINGS
The concrete foundations used when constructing walls and other structures.

GEO-TEXTILE MEMBRANE
A pervious sheet that can be laid over prepared ground to prevent perennial weed growth or act as a base for loose cobbles or decorative chippings.

GRAVEL BOARDS
Boards laid along the bottom of a fence to prevent it from rotting.

HA-HA
A stone-faced ditch, often with a fence at the bottom, which allows an uninterrupted view but prevents livestock from entering a park or garden.

HALVING JOINTS
A woodworking term whereby timbers are slotted so that they fit together at right angles to one another. Frequently used in structures such as pergolas or overheads.

HARDCORE
Crushed brick or stone used to form foundations.

HARD LANDSCAPING
All the hard surfaces of a garden, including paving, walling, fencing and steps as opposed to the planting or 'soft landscaping'.

HAUNCHING
A term used for setting bricks or stones in concrete, especially where they are used as a restraint at the edges of paths or other areas.

HEADERS
A term used for bricks or stone blocks laid crossways through a wall.

HIT AND MISS
Horizontal fencing boards set alternately behind and in front of the posts.

HOGGIN
A clay binder into which gravel is rolled when constructing paths.

JOIST HANGER
A metal shoe that is built into a wall to support overhead beams or similar structures.

PAVIOUR
A small but specific paving module such as a purpose-made brick or tile.

POINTING
The joints between brickwork that prevent water penetrating the vertical face. Pointing can be weathered, raked out or flush with the surface.

RAILWAY SLEEPERS
Known in the United States as railway ties, these are the balks of timber from railway tracks and can be used in the garden to construct steps, paving, raised beds and other features.

RENDERING
A cement finish applied to the vertical face of a wall or building.

SETTS
Small rectangular paving blocks, usually formed from granite or specialist precast concrete.

SHIMS
Thin wedges used for levelling decking or other timber surfaces.

SOFT LANDSCAPING
All the soft elements of a garden including lawns and planting of all kinds as opposed to the 'hard' structural elements.

STRETCHERS
A term used for bricks or stone blocks placed lengthways along a wall.

STRUCK
Removal of timber shuttering that is used to form *in situ* concrete walls or other structures once the concrete has hardened.

WEATHERED
A method of pointing brick walls in which the joints are angled to shed water easily.

YORK STONE
A greyish white sandstone, frequently used in Great Britain.

1 Jerry Harpur (Designer: Chris Rosmini, LA);

2 Vincent Motte (Bruno Carles);

5 S & O Mathews;

6–7 Clive Nichols (Designers: Graham Rose & John Keyes, Sunday Times Garden, Chelsea 1994);

8 Clive Nichols (Designer: Ernest Barnsley, Rodmarton Manor, Glos.);

9 *left* Jerry Harpur (Designer: Isabelle C. Green, Santa Barbara, CA);

9 *right* Jerry Harpur ('Ohinetahi', Christchurch, NZ);

10 *left* Vincent Motte;

10 *right* Jerry Harpur (Designer: Claus Scheinert);

11 *left* Andrew Lawson (Designer: Lynden B. Miller, NY);

11 *right* Andrew Lawson (Batsford Park, Glos.);

12 Jerry Harpur (Designer: Ragna Goddard, Conn.);

13 *above* Marianne Majerus;

13 *below* S & O Mathews;

14–15 Andrew Lawson (York Gate, Leeds);

16 Gary Rogers;

17 Jerry Harpur (Designer: Mel Light, Los Angeles, CA);

18 *above* Marianne Majerus (Heale House);

18 *below* Andrew Lawson;

19 Andrew Lawson (Gothic House, Oxfordshire);

20 *above* Brigitte Thomas;

20 *below* Gary Rogers;

21 *left* Jerry Harpur ('Dolwen' Cefn Coch, Llanrhaeder-ym-Mochnant);

21 *Right* Jerry Harpur (Villa Taylor, Marrakech);

22 Charles Mann (John Suarez, Andre Landscape Architects, Scottsdale, AZ);

23 *left* Christian Sarramon;

23 *right* Lanny Provo (Buddhist Monastery, Kyoto, Japan);

24 Jerry Harpur (Berry's Garden Company);

25 Andrew Lawson (Thuya Gardens, Maine);

26 Gary Rogers;

27 *above* Marianne Majerus;

27 *below* Jerry Harpur (Oehme & van Sweden Associates, Washington DC);

28 Michèle Lamontagne;

29 Clive Nichols (Designer: Lucy Gent);

30 *left* Gary Rogers/The Garden Picture Library;

30 *right* Andrew Lawson (RHS Gardens Wisley);

31 *left* Andrew Lawson (Courtesy of Beth Straus);

31 *right* Andrew Lawson (Designer: Bill Frederick);

32 Hotze Eisma/VT Wonen;

33 *left* Jerry Harpur (Designer: Mark Rumary, Yoxford, Suffolk);

33 *right* Jerry Harpur (Designer: Sonny Garcia, San Francisco, CA);

34 Lanny Provo (West End, Tortola, Virgin Islands);

35 *left* Clive Nichols (Designer: Jill Billington);

35 *right* Charles Mann (David Alford, Don Gaspar Compound B&B, Santa Fe, NM);

36 *left* Vincent Motte;

36 *right* Jerry Harpur (Designer: Keeyla Meadows, San Francisco, CA);

37 *left* Paul Ryan/International Interiors;

37 *right* Brigitte Thomas;

38 Jerry Harpur (Designer: Mel Light, Los Angeles, CA);

39 *left* Gary Rogers;

39 *right* Jerry Harpur (Designer: Thomasina Tarling);

40 Jerry Harpur (Ann Griot, Los Angeles, CA);

41 *left* Andrew Lawson;

41 *centre* Andrew Lawson (Designer: Rupert Golby);

41 *right* Jerry Harpur (Designer: Helen Yemm, London);

42 Christian Sarramon;

43 *above* Andrew Lawson (Courtesy of Lynden B. Miller);

43 *below* S & O Mathews;

44 Mick Hales (Dr Beisenkamp);

45 *above* Brigitte Thomas/The Garden Picture Library;

45 *below* Charles Mann;

46–47 S & O Mathews;

48 Charles Mann (Designer: Julia Berman, Eden Landscapes, Santa Fe, NM);

49 Gary Rogers;

50 Annette Schreiner (Designer: F. Bonnin);

51 *left* Gillian Darley/Edifice;

51 *right* Jacqui Hurst;

52 Brigitte Thomas;

53 *left* Gary Rogers;

53 *right* Mark Fiennes;

54 Christine Ternynck;

55 Neil Campbell-Sharp;

56 *above* Pippa Lewis/Edifice;

56 *below* Lanny Provo (Owner: Dennis Jenkins, Coconut Grove, Florida);

57 Charles Mann;

58 *left* Jerry Harpur (Designer: Isabelle C. Green, Santa Barbara);

58 *right* Charles Mann (Steve Martino, Martino and Associates, Phoenix, AZ);

59 *left* Lanny Provo;

59 *right* Lanny Provo (Coconut Grove, Florida);

60 Jerry Harpur;

61 *above* Jerry Harpur (Designer: Mel Light, Los Angeles, CA);

61 *below* Pippa Lewis/Edifice;

62 Jerry Harpur (Berry's Garden Company);

63 *above* Marianne Majerus;

63 *below* Mise au Point;

64 *left* Wildlife Matters;

64 *right* Clive Nichols (Designer: Sylvia Landsberg, Tudor Knot Garden, Southampton);

65 *left* Charles Mann (Mike Shoup, Antique Rose Emporium, Brennham, TX);

65 *right* Jerry Harpur/Elizabeth Whiting & Associates (Gail Jenkins, Melbourne, Victoria);

66 *left* Charles Mann;

66 *right* Steven Wooster/The Garden Picture Library (Designers: Duane Paul Design Team);

67 *above left* Marijke Heuff/The Garden Picture Library;

67 *above right* S & O Mathews;

67 *below right* Andrew Lawson;

68 *left* S & O Mathews;

68 *right* Brigitte Thomas;

69 *left* Jerry Harpur (Michael Wayman, Pymble, NSW);

69 *right* Gary Rogers;

70 *left* Gillian Darley/Edifice;

70 *right* Gary Rogers/The Garden Picture Library;

71 Tim Sandall (Designer: Barbara Hunt);

72 Pippa Lewis/Edifice;

73 Gary Rogers;

74 *left* Sarah Jackson/Edifice;

74 *right* Gillian Darley/Edifice;

75 *left* Charles Mann (Suzanne Crayson, Tesuque Meadows, Santa Fe, NM);

75 *right* Andrew Lawson;

76 Marianne Majerus (Woodpeckers);

77 Gary Rogers;

78 Christine Ternynck;

79 Neil Campbell-Sharp;

80 *above* S & O Mathews;

80 *below* Brigitte Thomas;

81 *left* Brigitte Thomas (Easgrove);

81 *right* Tim Griffiths/The Garden Picture Library;

82 *above* Marianne Majerus (Woodpeckers);

82 *below* Andrew Lawson (Glendurgan, Cornwall);

83 Brigitte Thomas;

84 Jerry Harpur ('Bolobek', Macedon, Australia);

85 Brigitte Thomas;

86 Brigitte Thomas (Hadsbeu);

87 *left* Gary Rogers;

87 *right* Charles Mann;

88–9 Steven Wooster (Designers: Mr & Mrs Anthony Huntington);

90 Beatrice Pichon-Clarisse;

91 Christian Sarramon;

92 *left* Christian Sarramon;

92 *right* Jerry Harpur (House of Pitmuies,

Acknowledgments

Guthrie-by-Forfar);
93 *left* Jerry Harpur (Designer: Bruce Kelly, New York);
93 *right* Andrew Lawson;
94 Christian Sarramon;
95 Claire de Virieu;
96 Roger Hyam/The Garden Picture Library;
97 *left* Charles Mann;
97 *right* Marianne Majerus;
98 *above* Gary Rogers;
98 *below* Marianne Majerus;
99 Michèle Lamontagne;
100 *left* Marianne Majerus (Heale House);
100 *right* Jerry Harpur (Bourton House, Gloucestershire);
101 *left* Beatrice Pichon-Clarissè (Designer: Guy Laine);
101 *right* Andrew Lawson (Courtesy of Frank Cabot, New York);
102 Brigitte Thomas;
103 Tim Street-Porter/Elizabeth Whiting & Associates;
104–5 Brigitte Thomas;
106 Neil Lorimer/Elizabeth Whiting & Associates;
107 Jerry Harpur (Designer: Jason Payne, London);
108 *left* Andrew Lawson (Courtesy of Frank Cabot, Quebec);
108 *above right* Jerry Harpur (Designer: Jim Matsuo, Los Angeles, CA);
108 *below right* Tim Street-Porter (Designer: Luis Barragan);
110 Andrew Lawson (Courtesy of Nancy & Bill Frederick, Delaware);
111 Jerry Harpur (Designer: Robert Watson, Christchurch, NZ);
112 *above* S & O Mathews;
112 *below* Marianne Majerus (Fairhaven Garden Trust);
113 S & O Mathews;
114 Jerry Harpur (Designer: Fred Watson, Alton, NH);
115 Brigitte Thomas;
116 Gary Rogers;
117 *left* Marianne Majerus;
117 *right* Gary Rogers;
118 *above* Jerry Harpur (Designer: Mark Rios, Los Angeles, CA);
118 *below* Jerry Harpur (Wyken Hall, Suffolk);
119 Andrew Lawson (Courtesy of Nancy & Bill Frederick, Delaware);
121 Charles Mann;
122 *above* Henri Del Olmo/Côté Sud/Elizabeth Whiting & Associates;
122 *below* Steven Wooster (Designer: Di Firth);
123 Fritz von der Schulenburg/The Interior Archive;

124 Christian Sarramon;
125 Karl Dietrich-Bühler/Elizabeth Whiting & Associates;
126 Steven Wooster (Designers: Bev & Ken Loader);
127 Lanny Provo (Zen Buddhist Garden, Kyoto, Japan);
128 *above* Jerry Harpur (Wollerton Old Hall, Shropshire);
128 *below* Andrew Lawson (Designer: Jim Keeling);
129 *left* Gary Rogers/The Garden Picture Library;
129 *right* Gary Rogers;
130 *left* Jean-Pierre Godeaut (Gilles Clement);
130 *right* Jerry Harpur ('Dolwen' Cefn Coch, Llanrhaeder-ym-Mochnant);
131 *left* Andrew Lawson (The Crossing House, Cambridge);
131 *right* Andrew Lawson;
132 *left* Fritz von der Schulenburg/The Interior Archive;
132 *right* Fritz von der Schulenburg/The Interior Archive;
133 Karl Dietrich-Bühler/Elizabeth Whiting & Associates;
134 Gary Rogers/The Garden Picture Library (Designer: Henk Weijers);
135 Claire de Virieu;
136 Wildlife Matters;
137 Geoffrey Frosh;
138–9 Neil Campbell-Sharp;
140 Clive Nichols (Keukenhoff Gardens, Holland);
141 Jerry Harpur (Designer: Beth Chatto, Elmstead Market, Essex);
142 Gary Rogers;
143 *left* Marianne Majerus;
143 *right* Andrew Lawson (Courtesy of Mrs Thomas Hall, Maine);
144 *left* S & O Mathews;
144 *right* Marianne Majerus (Designer: George Carter);
145 Mark Fiennes;
146 *left* Clive Nichols (Designer: Anthony Noel);
146 *right* Clive Nichols (Whatton, Leicestershire);
147 *above* Charles Mann;
147 *below* Vincent Motte;
148 *left* Marianne Majerus;
148 *right* Jerry Harpur ('Dolwen' Cefn Coch, Llanrhaeder-ym-Mochnant);
149 *left* Gary Rogers;
149 *right* Jacqui Hurst;
150 *left* Marianne Majerus;
150 *right* Gary Rogers;
151 *above* Vincent Motte;
151 *below* Marijke Heuff;
152 *left* Jacqui Hurst;
152 *right* Lynne Brotchie/The Garden Picture Library;

153 *left* Gary Rogers;
153 *right* Marianne Majerus (Artist: Jean-Pierre Raynaud, Gallerie Beaubourg, Vence.);
154 *above* Charles Mann (El Zaguan, Santa Fe Historical Society, Santa Fe, NM);
154 *below* S & O Mathews;
155 Jerry Harpur (Designer: Edwina von Gal, NY);
156 Wildlife Matters;
157 *left* Neil Campbell-Sharp;
157 *right* Andrew Lawson;
158 *left* Andrew Lawson;
158 *right* Lanny Provo (Yates Jungles Garden);
159 Jerry Harpur (Designer: Jim Matsuo, Los Angeles, CA);
160 Fritz von der Schulenburg/The Interior Archive;
161 *above* Fritz von der Schulenburg/The Interior Archive;
161 *below* Marijke Heuff (Walda Pairon);
162 Jerry Harpur (Designer: John Keyes, London);
163 *above* Christian Sarramon;
163 *below* Lanny Provo (Owner: Dennis Jenkins);
164 Vincent Motte;
165 *left* Steven Wooster (Designer: Anthony Paul);
165 *right* Marianne Majerus/The Garden Picture Library;
166 *above* Andrew Lawson;
166 *below* Gary Rogers;
167 *left* Gary Rogers;
167 *right* Jerry Harpur ('Stellenberg' Cape Town, RSA);
168 Jerry Harpur (Designer: Mark Rios, Los Angeles, CA);
169 Gary Rogers;
170 Gary Rogers;
171 Marianne Majerus (Designer: George Carter);
172 &173 Charles Mann;
174 Jacqui Hurst;
175 *above* Noel Kavanagh;
175 *below* Mark Fiennes;
176 *above* John Glover;
176 *below* S & O Mathews;
177 *left* S & O Mathews;
177 *right* Jerry Harpur (Gardens of Little Easton Lodge. Essex);
178 S & O Mathews;
179 *above* S & O Mathews;
179 *below* Jerry Harpur;
180 *above* S & O Mathews;
180 *below* Jacqui Hurst;
181 *left* S & O Mathews;
181 *right* Brigitte Thomas;
182 *left* Pippa Lewis/Edifice;
182 *right* Gary Rogers;
183 S & O Mathews.